The Love You Deserve

10 Keys
to
Perfect Love

Scott Peck

Grateful acknowledgement is made for permission to reprint the quotation from *The Essential Rumi,* translated by Coleman Barks and John Moyne. Originally published by Threshold Books, 139 Main Street, Brattleboro, VT 05301.

Grateful acknowledgement is also made for:
Quotation attributed to Albert Einstein.
Quotation from *Science and Health with Key to the Scriptures* by Mary Baker Eddy, published by The First Church of Christ, Scientist, Boston, MA 02115.
List of women in the National Women's Hall of Fame: 76 Fall Street, Seneca Falls, NY 13148 (315) 568-8060

Cover by Robert Howard.

Printed 00 99 98 ♥ 10 9 8 7 6 5 4 3

Publisher's Cataloging-in-Publication
(Provided by Quality Books, Inc)

Peck, Scott.
        The love you deserve : 10 keys to perfect love / Scott Peck. –
1st ed.
        p.cm.
        Preassigned LCCN: 97-94328
        ISBN: 0-9659976-3-4

        1. Love. 2. Intimacy (Psychology) 3. Interpersonal
communication. 4. Marriage–Handbooks,manuals,etc. I. Title

BF575.L8P43 1998   152.4'1
                              QBI97-41055

To

Shannon Peck

My wife, best friend, Soulmate, lover,
spiritual mentor, cherisher of my dreams,
and infinite partner

and

Kaia Phelps & Khanh Nguyen

My inherited, lovely daughters
May you each experience the love you deserve

and

Elaine & Sid
My mother and father,
for being an example of perfect love

Immense gratitude

Heartfelt thanks to each member of my invaluable review team: Patti Barnes, Sarah Battelle, Mary Jane Boyd, Virginia Byrd, Mark Harris, Chris & Kathy Faller, Bob & Sharon Griswold, Larry Jensen, Jill Lesly Jones, Janet Lynn, Justin & Katy McKinney, Patsy Neu, Khanh Nguyen, Shannon Peck, Kaia Phelps, Dan Powell, Dan & Nancy Price, Jim Redington, Rebecca Smith, Nan Tellier, and Shaun Michel Winn.

Additional gratitude to Collier Kaler, my publicist and friend, for her skill and sensitivity in helping to share this book with the universe.

*"The minute I heard my first love story
I started looking for you, not knowing
how blind that was.*

*Lovers don't finally meet somewhere.
They're in each other all along."*

Rumi

*"Problems cannot be solved at the
same level of awareness that created
them."*

Albert Einstein

*"No power can withstand divine
Love."*

Mary Baker Eddy

Contents

Awakening to Perfect Love

10 Keys to Perfect Love

Moving towards Perfect Love if you are...

Awakening

to

Perfect

Love

Self-quiz
Your ideal love-mate

Directions: This self-quiz will help you assess your present love consciousness. You'll have another opportunity to take this quiz at the end of the book.

The top 10 things I want in a love-mate:

1. _____

2. _____

3. _____

4. _____

5. _____

6. _____

7. _____

8. _____

9. _____

10. _____

Chapter 1

Your right
to perfect love

We face a tragedy in our love lives.

Over 50% of all marriages in the United States end in divorce. And how fulfilling are the remaining marriages?

> *When you think*
> *of your love life,*
> *can you raise your arms and heart*
> *in the joy of ecstasy?*

Far too few of us can.

Our love lives beg for transformation! We need a breakthrough in our love consciousness – a vision powerful enough to bring us into a new dimension of the love we deserve.

♦ If you are single, dating, or in the early stages of a love relationship, this book will be an empowering guide for understanding the love you deserve.

♦ If you are already enjoying a satisfying love relationship, this book will take you even higher.

♦ If you are struggling with an unsatisfying relationship, this book will illumine and liberate. The intense light of truth and love in these pages will bring your love life into inescapable clarity – and move you towards the love you deserve.

♦ If you think you are unworthy of being loved, or that it is too late and you will never truly be loved, let this book be a love letter to you personally.

***Come
enter the embrace
of
perfect love***

The universal song
of love

The vast majority of the songs of the world sing of our great desire to be loved.

Each of us – wherever we live on this planet – yearns to be loved by someone who cherishes us, believes in us, uplifts us, caresses our innermost soul, and empowers our entire being.

Can you envision yourself experiencing such love? Here is a taste of the love you deserve:

♦ A **bond of unity** with your love-mate so rich and empowering that it equals or exceeds the best friendship you have ever experienced.

♦ **Kindness and honesty** flowing so consistently from your love-mate that you experience liberation from fear, guilt, condemnation, or anxiety in your love life.

♦ Your **innermost dreams cherished** and nurtured so fully by your love-mate that you feel empowered to express all that you yearn to be.

♦ **Genuine equality** in every nook of your love life – in lovemaking, decision-making, lifepath pursuit, socializing, finances, and daily living.

♦ The delight and satisfaction of **perpetual intimacy** – and a deep assurance of your love-mate's unconditional love.

- ♦ Such loving, **powerful listening** from your love-mate that you feel understood and esteemed to the core of your heart.
- ♦ The exhilaration of **loving yourself perfectly**.
- ♦ Experiencing a love that flows out from **pure spirituality**.

Can you
envision
this possibility?

When we fail to envision

Less than 100 years ago, women did not have the right to vote.

Think of the mentality then. The vast majority of women and men did not *envision* that a woman deserved to vote. It had not entered *consciousness* as a possibility, much less a "right."

It was not until 1920 – after great personal struggles, sacrifices, and hard work by a few visionary pioneers – that women were granted the right to vote in the United States.

"Granted" the right! Who granted this right? When were men granted the right to vote? Who granted men this right?

Do you see what truly took place? A great shift took place – in *consciousness*. Even though a few women understood and advocated this new idea, it didn't become a right until it was accepted in collective consciousness. Today, this right is recognized and cherished almost universally.

***Don't underestimate
the power of
collective consciousness
once it accepts a new right***

If you heard on today's news that the U.S. Congress was voting on legislation to repeal a woman's right to vote, would you believe it?

Of course not! Why? Because a woman's right to vote is now firmly established in consciousness.

American society went through the same expansion of consciousness with racial equality. Would the U.S. Congress today consider a bill to re-legalize slavery? No! Yet not that long ago, collective consciousness was blind to this right as well.

Here is the big question:

Weren't these rights always legitimate?

Of course they were! But we first had to *envision* them as rights before they could become a reality.

We had to admit the *possibility*!

This is exactly what needs to take place today in our intimate love lives. Our sense of love needs to expand exponentially. We are being lifted to a vastly higher consciousness of love.

We are all being called forth – in consciousness – to recognize our right *to perfect love*

Like the right to equality, this right to perfect love already exists – within each of us – waiting to be acknowledged and experienced.

Looking back 100 years from now, let our sons and daughters not wonder:

> *"How could they have been so ignorant of their right to perfect love?"*

Perfect love *is* possible

The dawning of a higher idea is often met with skepticism, but the issue is not whether perfect love is possible. The real issue is:

> *"What is perfect love and how can I experience it immediately?"*

We must open thought to this right in order for the love we deserve to become visible.

> **You are not likely to experience**
> **love**
> **greater than your**
> **consciousness**
> **can**
> **conceive**

The quality of the love you experience is a direct outcome of the quality of your thought and the standard of love you accept for yourself.

- ♦ If you think that inequality in love is tolerable, you will experience it.
- ♦ If you think your dreams are less worthy than your love-mate's dreams, that is the way your dreams will be treated.
- ♦ If you think that perfect love is impossible, you won't be open to experience it.

If you doubt that you can experience perfect love, this doubt is simply the result of the present standard of love you have accepted for yourself – not a fixed reality of your love-life.

The only thing that can hold you back from perfect love is your own thinking. You can never be deprived of perfect love by another person, or any condition.

Open your mind to this possibility.

Allow yourself the gift of admitting to your own thought:

I
deserve
to be
perfectly loved!

How long will it take?

Perfect love comes forth when consciousness opens the door

It took me 50 years to open myself to the love I deserved. I'm astounded that I could have lived so long in ignorance of my right to be perfectly loved.

Today I live in the utter heart and joy of perfect love with my wife, best friend, lover, Soulmate, colleague, confidant, mentor, and spiritual partner, Shannon.

This entire book flows out from our relationship. My desire is that every individual in the universe experience the liberation, power, and joy of the love we experience every day.

I always knew that I deserved such love. So did Shannon. In our ignorance, however, we both thought it would happen naturally when we married.

Well, it didn't. Each of us endured difficult, hurtful earlier marriages. We had assumed, naively, that we would be completely loved when we married. We weren't prepared for less. In our love ignorance, neither of us had a clue that perfect love was a *right*. Consequently, we didn't know how to make decisions that would bring perfect love into our lives.

Through great struggles and deep prayers for many years, each of us, separately, gained higher mental ground. Our separate marriages led to divorces and the consequent struggle to see ourselves as undamaged and worthwhile.

This book is the outcome – the story – of the consciousness that led each of us to each other and the awareness of our right to be loved perfectly. Today, neither of us could imagine settling for less!

You have an immense opportunity that we didn't have. You can learn what it means to be loved perfectly by allowing this book to lift you to the consciousness of the love you deserve.

Each of us deserves such love.

No one is excluded.

If perfect love
seems unimaginable to you,
open
your consciousness
to a new level
of love

The Big Picture
The love you deserve

In order to make the transition to a new love reality, we need a bold and clear model – a model etched so clearly in our consciousness that we have no doubt where we are going or what we deserve.

If you are not yet aware of your right to perfect love, the following chapters will awaken you as you feel the truth of these ten keys illumine your inner worth. The love *you* deserve includes:

- A bond of unity
- Kindness + Honesty
- Cherishing each other's dreams
- Genuine equality
- Listening to the heart
- Perpetual intimacy
- Empowering manhood
- Self-empowered womanhood
- Loving yourself perfectly
- Loving out from Spirituality

Before plunging into these powerful keys, take the self-quiz on the next page. It will help you take stock of your present love consciousness.

The Love You Deserve
Self-quiz

Directions: If you currently have a love-mate, circle the number that best describes your relationship. If you don't have a love-mate at this time, circle the lowest rating you are willing to accept with any love-mate-to-be. (Note: an additional copy of this quiz is in the addendum.)

1. I feel a bond of unity with my love-mate:

    1   2   3   4   5   6   7   8   9   10
    Not at all   To some degree   Completely

2. I am treated with consistent kindness and honesty by my love-mate:

    1   2   3   4   5   6   7   8   9   10
    Not at all   To some degree   Completely

3. My love-mate cherishes my dreams:

    1   2   3   4   5   6   7   8   9   10
    Not at all   To some degree   Completely

4. I experience genuine equality with my love-mate in all aspects of our relationship:

    1   2   3   4   5   6   7   8   9   10
    Not at all   To some degree   Completely

5. My love-mate listens to my heart:

    1   2   3   4   5   6   7   8   9   10
    Not at all   To some degree   Completely

6. I experience perpetual intimacy with my love-mate:

    1   2   3   4   5   6   7   8   9   10
    Not at all   To some degree   Completely

7. My love-mate honors and supports empowering manhood:

    1   2   3   4   5   6   7   8   9   10
    Not at all   To some degree   Completely

8. My love-mate honors and supports empowered womanhood:

    1   2   3   4   5   6   7   8   9   10
    Not at all   To some degree   Completely

9. I love myself perfectly:

    1   2   3   4   5   6   7   8   9   10
    Not at all   To some degree   Completely

10. I am loving out from spirituality:

    1   2   3   4   5   6   7   8   9   10
    Not at all   To some degree   Completely

Self-Rating

The love you deserve

Total Score: _____ divided by 10 = _____

1-2   Love vacuum. Time for radical revision or new possibilities.

3-4   Minimal love. Time to set higher standards.

5-6   Survivable love. Is this acceptable to you for the rest of your life?

7-8   Decent love. Why not go for the gold? What would move you to a 10?

9-10   Perfect love. Rejoice!

10 keys

to

Perfect Love

Chapter 2

A
bond
of unity

Think of the most perfect friendship you have ever had.

What made it – or makes it – so good?

Go ahead. Write down what describes your best ever friendship:

My best ever friendship
included...

- ♦ _____
- ♦ _____
- ♦ _____
- ♦ _____
- ♦ _____
- ♦ _____

Think of all the ways this question will be answered by those who read this book. Collectively, you will be describing the richness and depth of true friendship.

In truth, it's not hard to identify what creates a true friendship.

In true friendship...

♦ We are richly valued – for who we currently are.

♦ We feel safe to be ourselves without guilt, shame, or manipulation.

♦ We share our feelings, dreams, and needs with consistent honesty, open-ness, and kindness with each other.

♦ We laugh easily and freely.

♦ We are listened to thoroughly.

♦ We are not judged or condemned.

♦ We care about each other's well-being as much as our own.

The benefits and joy of a true bond of friendship are extraordinary. No games. No need to impress each other. Freedom to be our inner selves. Supported in exploring our dreams. Mental comfort. Esteem. Self-worth.

Can you envision your most intimate love-relationship including such a wonderful bond of unity?

This is your *right!*

Perfect love is rooted and grounded in a bond of unity – a deep friendship. You cannot experience perfect love if you sacrifice this bond.

A bond of friendship is the core of perfect love

When you say to your inner self, *"I deserve a bond of friendship with my love-mate and I will accept no less,"* your love-life will take a dramatic step forward.

Let's look squarely at one of the top derailers of the love you deserve.

The deceit
of physical attraction

We are hypnotized by sex.

Second by second, we are subjected to a mental onslaught of sexually-oriented ads, dialogue, and pictures – in magazines, on TV, in movies and videos, in the songs we listen to, and in the conversations we hear around us.

We are so mesmerized that we are duped into a craving for the beautiful pin-up woman or hunk-of-man. We dream, yearn...dream, yearn...and dream, yearn... until this love desire becomes a fixation. And we think this is normal!

It's normal, all right, like divorce, tears, abuse, and destroyed relationships have become normal.

Each of us deserves so much more than a shallow relationship based primarily on physicality and sex.

Of course we deserve to be loved – richly and passionately – in all ways. But physical attraction cannot sustain genuine love. A love relationship based *primarily* on physical attraction has devastating consequences:

♦ Who you are in your inner soul is likely to remain unknown, smothered, and forever unexpressed – because you may be afraid to risk losing your relationship by revealing your true self.

♦ The relationship is likely to end, at some point, in one of you being physically attracted to someone else. One of you will end up hurt.

♦ There is likely to be tension, anger, frustration, disillusionment, and fighting because a physical relationship cannot bear the stress of all that naturally rises to the surface in an intimate relationship.

"But I want passionate love!" you cry. *"I want fireworks and sizzle!"*

And you deserve it!

Even better, you can have it!

But it won't provide lasting happiness without solid friendship as the base.

> ***Physical attraction***
> ***without friendship***
> ***cannot sustain***
> ***the heart and soul***
> ***of genuine love***

This is the great deceit of relationships that hope to build from sex-up rather than friendship-up. Genuine friendship is not something that can simply be tacked on after a physical relationship is in full swing.

Friendship first

Friendship first is the guaranteed win-win strategy for your love life.

When friendship evolves into passionate love, it has the rich substance that fires pleasure deep within our soul – and this pleasure is enduring.

When friendship does not evolve into a love relationship, you still end up with a new friend. Either way, you will feel satisfied *and* empowered.

Be honest with yourself. Without friendship, what chance does a love relationship have of being truly fulfilling and enduring?

None!

You deserve the great pleasure of passionate love that blossoms *within* a bond of friendship.

***Friendship first
opens
a relationship
to its fullest potential***

But what happens if a potential love-mate wants to zing into passion-mode and come back to friendship later? Or expresses no interest whatsoever in a bond of friendship?

Don't compromise! This is the exact moment – the turning point – that will determine the quality of love you will experience.

The quality of love-mates we attract is a mirror of our own love standards

If you don't set the standard, in your own mind, that a bond of friendship with your love-mate is essential, it won't be there.

By taking this stand, you may fear that you will give up all possibility of ever being loved, or that you will be too lonely. It is so tempting to compromise – because we all want to be loved so badly, and right now!

Don't sell yourself short!

You are worthy of perfect love.

Affirm to yourself:

"I am deeply worthy of being loved perfectly

I want a bond of friendship with my love-mate and I will accept no less!"

When you take a stand for a bond of friendship in your love life, the love-mate you truly deserve will step forward – because that's who you will attract.

Finding a love-mate is not a question of time, place, looks, talent, or opportunity

–

It's a question of **consciousness**

Let me tell you about myself.

My own love story

This is what I finally experienced in my own love life when I woke up:

**When you take a mental stand
for perfect love,
your love experience
will rise
to your new expectations**

After I was divorced, I felt unworthy. I felt that I would never experience the genuine love I thought would be a natural part of my life. Even though it was an enormous relief to be finished with an unhappy marriage, I knew I had a lot of love to give.

Why shouldn't I be loved as richly as I knew I could give love?

I came to a revealing conclusion: I would rather remain single forever than ever again be unhappily married. I knew right then that I had inwardly crossed a key mental mile-marker. I had decided that if I were ever to remarry (which, to be honest, I doubted), my needs and dreams deserved to be richly valued and loved. I thought to myself:

**"I
deserve
to be
well loved!"**

This idea empowered my entire inner life and sense of self-esteem. It felt good to love myself enough to claim such love.

Over the next months, this idea kept strengthening within me until, finally, in the privacy of my own consciousness, it exploded in light. I thought to myself, *"This is even bigger than deserving to be well loved."*

I deserve to be perfectly loved!

This was astonishing to me. Never, in the first 50 years of my life, had I envisioned this idea – this *right* – to be perfectly loved!

I felt the power of this idea so keenly that I knew right then that it was inevitable that I would experience perfect love – even though there was no one special in my love life at that time. I was as sure of my right to perfect love as I was sure that the sun would rise the next day.

I knew that time and circumstances had nothing to do with it. My consciousness had risen to an entirely new dimension. I was absolutely sure of success in experiencing my right to the perfect love I deserved.

Several weeks later, while I was conducting a workshop on unconditional love, one of the participants raised her hand to answer a question. I didn't know her, but I immediately knew that she would play a powerful role in my life.

To my regret, I was told that she was married, so I didn't contact her. Weeks later, however, I learned that she was actually divorced. I called her and with simple honesty, said: "I met you recently at a workshop. I don't know if you remember me (she did), but I felt led to call you. I think we need to know each other." She was rushing out to an appointment when I called, and asked if I would call back.

Well, I didn't. Even though I had come to the conclusion that I deserved to be perfectly loved, was I right to intuit so strongly that this was the person? As some of you may understand, living through a marriage where I was not esteemed or cherished, my feeling of self-worth was still recovering. I was also just leaving for a three-week photo-shoot in Turkmenistan and Uzbeckistan in Central Asia, with a fellow photographer and friend.

During those next three weeks – completely isolated from the rest of the world or any communications – I continued to feel the clear presence of my new-found right to be perfectly loved.

It was a quiet awareness in my consciousness. I now knew that this right was inherent within me. It was such a powerful sense of love that I felt like I was *already* experiencing perfect love. I'll never forget it. This is what it taught me:

The consciousness
of perfect love
precedes
the
event

When I returned to work, there was a message waiting – would I please call her.

We met that weekend – the beginning of a bond of unity that expanded to the perfect love I now enjoy with Shannon, my extraordinary wife and love-mate.

Shannon's love story

Here's is Shannon's version of our love story – in her own words.

After my ex-husband left me, after eighteen years of marriage, my self-esteem was at an all-time low. I was devastated, even though it had never been a happy marriage. The pain was almost unbearable. My needs were overwhelming.

I began working to heal myself, working each afternoon in my office, while my phone was quiet. I'll never forget the first afternoon I did this.

When, for the millionth time, I felt prompted to feel devastated, I went into a mode of bold and powerful affirmations based on my deeply held understanding that I am spiritual.

My affirmations specifically challenged and replaced unspiritual thoughts I was thinking about myself. Whatever I needed at the most fundamental emotional level, I turned into a powerful affirmation. All my affirmations came forth from my highest sense of spiritual truth.

For example, I boldly declared to my consciousness such truths as:

♦ *Love is seeking me out and claiming me as its own, saying, "You are mine! You belong to me!"*

♦ *Because Love is ever-present, I am always in the full, living presence of Love – and I know it and feel this love here and now and everywhere.*

♦ *The entire area of my consciousness that appears to be so dark is actually filled with great light. I am in this light. I live in the splendor of this glorious moment!*

♦ *Because I am spiritual, I am singled out by infinite Love and labeled worthy of praise and adoration. I feel and see Love rejoicing over me, celebrating me.*

♦ *Divine Love is announcing my great goodness to all mankind, and all mankind is responding to me with love. I see Love manifesting to me in infinite ways right now. I feel totally secure and safe in this Love.*

♦ *Because I am spiritual, Love has a wonderful plan for me that names me in the plan as absolutely essential. Love makes sure I am aware of this.*

♦ *I feel Love loving, embracing, providing, upholding, encouraging, and directing me every step, every moment.*

♦ *I am guided, comforted, and protected by Love. I feel secure with all life's changes because Love is the governing, intelligent power of my life.*

♦ *Because I am spiritual, I am being husbanded by God. God is my husband and He is naming me as his glorious wife, worthy of His love. Together, we share in this radiant light of beauty.*

♦ *I am never alone. I am always experiencing the wonderful love of my infinitely loving Husband.*

Sometimes, as I stated these and many other affirmations, I would giggle and laugh out loud. These affirmations were so far from my experience that it seemed ridiculous to state them as true.

However, I was accustomed to going to the divine core and making bold statements of Truth – and later seeing their supremacy and power rule the situation. I trusted my spiritual reasoning implicitly.

Within a short while, the expression of Love began to fill my life. A couple of wonderful men appeared in my life, one of whom I thought was "Mr. Right." Another was Scott.

There was something unusual, however, about my friendship with Scott – it was a true bond of unity. I could feel how deeply he cherished whatever was most important to me.

Because of his honoring, my fears and doubts about being committed began to wash away. New hope rose within me. I slowly came to trust the genuineness and quality of Scott's love as the true manifestation of my spiritual affirmations.

I told "Mr. Right" my heart's true knowing. I needed to let my relationship with Scott unfold in the magnificence of what I knew was answered prayer.

I know that Scott and I found each other through divine Love, the source of all love. I found that I could completely trust divine Love's law of attraction and cohesion to govern my entire life – including my love life.

Establishing friendship
with a
potential love-mate

"What can I do to ensure that this relationship will be grounded on true friendship?"

That's the question I asked myself when Shannon and I became instant friends, began dating, and it became obvious that the relationship could easily evolve into much, much more.

Even as I wondered how this relationship would unfold, a deep truth was speaking to me in my private consciousness:

**If this friendship
is meant to become love,
nothing can stop it**

—

**If this friendship
is meant to be only
friendship,
I will cherish that friendship**

This is a powerful affirmation. It unites us with Love itself. I relaxed in the consciousness of this truth. I knew I would experience perfect love at some point in my life because I knew now that this was my inherent right. I did not need to worry whether it would be with Shannon.

I relished the wonderful friendship we were experiencing and I knew that I could no longer settle for less in any love-partnership.

What happened next was phenomenal. Our friendship grew to awesome power for each of us. We experienced the depth of a bond of unity:

- ◆ We spoke to each other with complete honesty and openness, no matter how embarrassed we felt. We didn't hide our feelings about anything. This was a joint decision early on.
- ◆ There were no games. No playing with each other's feelings. No manipulation.
- ◆ We listened deeply to each other's feelings, needs, and desires – by the hours.
- ◆ There was extraordinary and reliable kindness.
- ◆ We laughed freely and continuously, enjoying the freedom of our friendship.
- ◆ We honored each other's accomplishments and life-insights.
- ◆ We didn't judge each other. We both felt deeply valued for who we really were.
- ◆ Through an unconditional respect for each other's individuality, we discussed our inner dreams.

Can you envision how good this felt?

As weeks passed in the enjoyment of this friendship, it was obvious that a love-partnership was developing and deepening.

What would happen to our friendship during this transition?

Holding on to friendship
when
love takes over

Can friendship and romance develop simultaneously?

I knew a turning point had arrived as the love that Shannon and I felt for each other grew more dominant. Would our friendship now change? Would it be compromised?

As friends, Shannon and I felt total liberation at sharing our feelings. We had nothing to lose. We were living within a bond of friendship. That is what we both needed and wanted. Now that love was surfacing, it became more challenging to be honest. I found myself privately thinking:

"If I reveal my true feelings, Shannon might think I'm stupid or weak and I may lose this opportunity to be loved."

This thinking, of course, if acted out, would have quickly destroyed the bond of our open friendship.

Deep within my consciousness, I recognized that I would rather lose Shannon as a love-partner than have a love-relationship, however beautiful, devoid of genuine honesty.

I felt both empowered and scared feeling this way, but there was no other true choice for me. So I spoke the truth, expecting more than once, that the truth would cause our budding love to wither.

For example, during this period of rapidly growing friendship, I had felt frustrated in my occupation. Yet I feared that if I shared this with Shannon, our potential love relationship might be lost. I was afraid this would make me unattractive to her.

But our friendship was too important to sacrifice. So I shared my feelings openly, revealing my real inner self. I was shocked by her reaction. She loved me more! And she deeply appreciated my openness.

I had answered the question: *"Am I willing to give up friendship for love?"* with a resounded *"No!"* I wanted *both* and I knew that I deserved both.

The immense closeness of our friendship empowered each of us. As we each encouraged more of such liberating honesty, we found greater and greater unity.

I can't begin to tell you the exhilaration of experiencing this love within the context of a bond of unity. It is not just that our love grew stronger. Our friendship flourished just as powerfully. We felt the liberation of friendship *and* love.

This is the love *you* deserve. And it begins in your consciousness.

**You alone
set the standard
for the quality
of your
love life**

Chapter 3

Kindness + Honesty

Kindness + honesty
unite us
with our love-mate
at the level
of Soul

Kindness combined with honesty is awesome in its power to liberate love.

It says to each love-mate:

"You are emotionally safe in my love
at all times and you can depend on
my kindness and honesty."

Think of kindness + honesty as a combined force that needs to be expressed *simultaneously*.

Why simultaneously?

For two good reasons:

♦ Without kindness, honesty stings our heart and causes us to retreat from love.

♦ Without honesty, however, kindness feels empty and untrustworthy and leads away from intimacy.

Expressed *simultaneously*, kindness + honesty bring out and uplift the love we deserve.

Envision what your life would feel like if your love-mate treated you with consistent kindness *and* honesty:

♦ You would know what your love-mate was feeling, experiencing, and thinking at the most intimate level of your love-mate's identity.

♦ You would be able to reveal your desires, feelings, hopes, fears, and needs to your love-mate in an environment of support and trust.

♦ Feeling the immense security of consistent kindness, you would feel more and more able to reveal vulnerable feelings and half-thought hopes or ideas. You would feel emotionally secure to be your complete inner self.

♦ You would enjoy the freedom and exhilaration of exploring and sharing parts of yourself never before ventured.

♦ Your love-mate would also feel free to be open and natural – without fear of attack, ridicule, or abuse.

This is what love-mates in perfect love expect, contribute, and enjoy.

This is the love you deserve!

Is consistent kindness + honesty possible?

It sure is!

Is it common? Unfortunately, no.

Why?

- ◆ Because so many love-mates are conditioned to accept so much less.
- ◆ Because so many love-mates have themselves been treated with such unkindness that they have never experienced consistent kindness.
- ◆ Because so many love-mates have never learned how to be kind or honest.
- ◆ Because so many love-mates have discovered that they can get away with unkindness and lack of honesty without serious consequences.

The tide in love relationships, however, is turning. Lovers are waking up. Abuse of a love-mate is now a waving flag of an outdated mode of thinking.

***Unkindness
and
lack of honesty
are abuse***

Until you understand that unkindness and lack of honesty are abuse, you are likely to tolerate, accept, and experience them.

We must rise in our consciousness of perfect love to see that we deserve to experience the peace and support of sustained kindness + honesty. Anything less than this is a sham on love. Let us not be fooled. Good looks, wealth, dazzling opportunities, and sizzling moments do not overcome the internal havoc and disaster of unkindness or lack of honesty.

> *"Come on Scott, don't you and Shannon ever act with unkindness to each other?"*

Shannon and I are so grateful to no longer be in past marriages which included unkindness that we treasure the kindness we experience with each other. It's essential to us. We count on it. We are committed to it.

Our kindness stems from our great love for each other and our view of kindness as the natural expression of divine Love. To be unkind violates our deepest understanding of who we are as expressions of Love.

We falter, of course, and there are times when we hurt each other's feelings, but not often – and never deliberately. On stressful days, we stretch to be kind and respectful – even as we work through emotions.

We usually sense when one of us does or says something that hurts the other, and we act quickly to correct our words or actions rather than let hurt take on a life of its own. We seek to discover why the other is hurt, and we make sure our larger love for each other is always acknowledged.

We are also willing to change our behavior if this is what it takes for the other to feel loved, but we are also true to ourselves. This is the fine balance where kindness + honesty *combined* have great healing power.

We work to rise above the negative thinking that would let us wallow in hurt, frustration, or anger. We know that holding on to such feelings holds back our creativity, our joy, our life purpose, and our love. We have learned not to be self-destructive. Here's a typical example.

While we were engaged, Shannon had been thinking about getting her first computer. She was leaning towards a Macintosh because of its reputation for being easy to use.

I tried to steer her towards an IBM-compatible because that's where I was experienced. We had several discussions where we respectfully (I thought) disagreed.

Well, one evening, Shannon phoned and announced that she had decided to buy the Macintosh – and she asked me not to try to talk her out of it. In fact, she said she felt like a little flower being crushed by a ten-ton steamroller on this issue.

I was caught off-guard by her strong feelings.

It is at such a love-juncture that perfect love needs to excel. What seems like a simple issue can escalate into a power struggle, a control issue, or a feeling of alienation.

I immediately told Shannon that I honored her right to make whatever decision she wanted – and that I understood the appeal of the Macintosh. I listened as she explained that she had just come out of an 18-year marriage of domination on such decision-making. This computer choice was one of her first decisions to make on her own.

I felt terrible. I had completely underestimated the impact of Shannon's previous marriage on her well-being. Instantly, I wholeheartedly switched sides. I knew that her right to make her own decisions was the central issue, and I cherished her right to be independent. Of course, I was also eager to distance myself from being compared to a ten-ton steamroller!

I told her that my motivation in suggesting an IBM-compatible computer was not to control the decision, but to help us more intimately connect our lives by sharing compatible computers and equipment. My motivation was to be as completely unified with Shannon as possible, and I told her this.

Sensing my depth of honoring for her, Shannon also switched sides, realizing the choice was not about control and domination. My kindness + honesty spoke volumes to her and cut away a history of being controlled.

The issue was never a computer. The real issue – to Shannon – was her right to make her own decisions. The real issue – to me – was my desire to be as unified as possible with Shannon.

Our kindness + honesty brought these real issues to the surface to be known – and healed. Anger or frustration would have buried the real issues and our love would have paid the price. We happily share compatible computer systems today – and Shannon made the final decision.

There are many ways to bring the empowering combination of kindness + honesty into your love life. One way is to ask a very simple question:

"What are you thinking, honey?"

This powerful, delicate question instantly shows your desire to connect with your love-mate.

It asks for honesty from your love-mate, but if asked with kindness, it opens a path for sharing. It enables an instant uniting of hearts.

Even with kindness, however, this question is so honest and open that it can catch a love-mate off-guard. One might feel:

"If my love-mate knew what I was really thinking right now, I'd be in trouble! I'm not emotionally prepared to share my thoughts."

Yet here is the exact moment where kindness + honesty can come to the table with great healing power.

For example, suppose that you have been working overtime and you just sat down in the living room with your love-mate, not thinking too seriously about anything, but you sense that your love-mate is thinking deeply about something, so you ask: "What are you thinking honey?"

And suppose your love-mate responds:

"I'm feeling that you have been distant and wrapped up in your own life. It's as if you don't care and I don't matter. I am not feeling loved."

And you're thinking:

"Oh great. I just sat down to unwind. If I had known this was coming, I would have stayed in the other room."

This is one of those significant turning-points in a love relationship where your response will make a huge difference to the quality of your love life.

Let's look at three possible answers to your love-mate's words:

Answer 1:

> *"What the heck do you expect me to do, stop doing my job well? I'm under a lot of stress. Get off my back!"*

Answer 2:

> *"Honey, I'm buried to my eyeballs in this project. I have no choice. Can't this wait?"*

Answer 3:

> *"Sweetie, I love you. I'm sorry you feel this way. I have a lot of things on my mind. Let's take a moment to share our thoughts together."*

You can easily chart the impact of answers 1, 2, and 3 on the love relationship.

Answer 1: This answer is honest, but with harshness, frustration, and anger. Even if given in the first flush of feelings, this answer slams the door on real love. It raises all the defense shields. How many times can you or your love-mate survive this answer and still consider yourselves as "loving" each other?

Answer 2: This answer is honest, but without caring. It shows a complete focus of thought on yourself and excludes your love-mate's needs. Without kindness, how often will your love-mate want to ask or answer the question, "What are you thinking, honey?" Goodbye intimacy.

Answer 3: This answer is honest *and* kind. Rather than an emotional knee-jerk response, it shows compassion for your love-mate and a recognition that discussion is needed to solidify your love. It may be emotionally difficult to come up with this answer from your heart, but it is worth whatever internal struggle it takes to get to this depth of love.

*Every single time you
act with
kindness + honesty
you increase your skill with this
powerful force
and
uplift your love life*

It's not easy
to come out of our shells

Love-mates often exist together like two ships passing in the night – unseen and unknown.

It takes great kindness to navigate the waters of deep intimacy and bring us out of our shells. It also takes great honesty, but this very honesty reveals the emeralds waiting to be discovered in the depths of each other's love.

When these gems are left unmined, love withers. I know! In my previous marriage, I did a lousy job of speaking out openly with my feelings. I felt extremely vulnerable. When I did muster the strength to speak out from my inner heart, I often felt scorned, ridiculed, or emotionally ignored. Behind the listening, I felt a hidden wave of anger and disgust to my responses.

Not too surprisingly, I retreated into the privacy of my own mental shell.

As any good Star Trek fan will understand, when you have to divert most of your life-energy to your shields (defense mechanisms), you don't have full power for your main systems. I was operating at minimal life-power.

Today, I am married to Shannon – and what a difference! Because of her consistent kindness and encouraging love, I now speak forcefully and openly from the heart. I even have this book as evidence!

What Shannon did was extremely liberating to me. More than anything else, she created an environment of great kindness. Whatever I shared from the heart was cherished, listened to, and discussed with great honoring.

You will hear more about this in the next chapter, *Cherishing each other's dreams.*

How did Shannon do this?

Primarily with kindness.

Shannon expressed such easy acceptance, joy, honesty, spiritual honoring, and laughter that my heart melted into openness. I found myself more and more able to reveal my inner self because of her kindness + honesty.

If you love roses, you prepare the best possible soil, cherish each tiny little bud, and smile with gratitude with each blossom.

Let us
nurture and cherish
our love-mate
at each stage
of
budding and blooming

The consequences of
unkindness and lack of honesty

The consequences of unkindness and lack of honesty are devastating to love:

- ♦ We feel disconnected from our love-mate.
- ♦ We feel uncertain.
- ♦ We live only with the shell of the person we call our "love-mate" without knowing what that shell really contains.
- ♦ We lead increasingly separate lives emotionally and intellectually.
- ♦ We are forced to seek out friends to share our pent-up feelings and needs.
- ♦ However immoral, we may be attracted to other relationships that promise true intimacy.
- ♦ We clam up our true thoughts and feelings for fear of ridicule, abuse, or disinterest.
- ♦ We raise our shields in self-defense of our fragile dreams and needs.
- ♦ We feel a well of resentment, hurt, and anger escalate within our consciousness and spill over to our love life.
- ♦ We don't feel loved!

These terrible consequences are not easily undone. If a love-mate treats us with unkindness in one instance, how will we know when the next bite or attack will come? If a love-mate is not open – or lies on even one issue – how can you believe there will be truth on other issues?

Love is so fragile.

Our dreams, needs, feelings, and ideas are like tiny roots that need tender nourishment.

Nothing nourishes
love
like the
combined force
of
kindness + honesty

When kindness + honesty are abused

With so many marriages ending in divorce, kindness + honesty may seem an impossibility in our love-lives. But shouldn't this jolt us awake?

We need a massive shift in consciousness and behavior if genuine love is to survive. That's what this book – and chapter – is about.

Those love-mates who blame, condemn, criticize, have temper fits, swear at their love mates, demean their love mates, or physically threaten their love-mates will likely recoil at the words in this chapter – in either shame or dismissal.

Those love-mates experiencing such blame, condemnation, criticism, temper fits, demeaning language, actions, or threats will read the message of this chapter and likely turn to their mental pillows with hidden tears.

My compassion for any love-mate lacking an environment of kindness + honesty runs deep. It motivates this book.

- ♦ Consistent kindness + honesty are essential ingredients in your love life.

- ♦ You should accept no less than consistent kindness + honesty with your love-mate.

- ♦ If you are the one not expressing kindness + honesty, face down this enemy or you are likely to lose not only your self-respect, but your love-mate as well.

The light
of
kindness + honesty
cannot
be stopped

It is not easy to draw the line in love. But a *pattern* of unkindness does extensive damage to our love lives and cannot be ignored.

This is not the love you deserve. You deserve a barrel full of pure kindness + honesty.

Let me explain.

What's stored in
your barrel?

A powerful mentor once told me a story:

> *"Imagine a large barrel, full of oil. What would come out if someone knocked a hole in the side of this barrel."*

Obviously, oil.

> *What would come out if the barrel were full of water?*

Obvious again, water.

**Now envision
your consciousness as a barrel,
full of whatever feelings and thoughts
are in your thinking**

Suppose, for example, that your consciousness is half full of love and half full of anger and resentment. And then your love-mate comes along and asks you a tough question. What will come out?

Inevitably, love *and* anger and resentment.

Here is the healing insight:

**Your response
to any event
exists
prior
to the event**

Now envision a different outcome. Suppose that early this morning in your quiet meditation, you worked to release all anger, fear, and doubt clinging for life in your consciousness because you understood their destructive nature if left in your barrel. You did your best to have nothing but kindness + honesty in your consciousness. You recognized that this would empower you, your love-mate, and the entire world you encountered today.

And then the events of the day unfold. What will come out as you respond to these events?

Of course, kindness + honesty!

This is potent information for two love-mates. It means that if we take the time to fill our *consciousness* with kindness + honesty, this is what will come out, even when we are caught off guard.

As we fill our barrel with love, our *consciousness* becomes an enormous defense system – already established – against reacting negatively to events.

Realistically, is this possible? It sure is!

True or false? Some people just get angry. That's the way they are. They can't change.

FALSE: We are each in charge of our thoughts and actions. Old habits of reacting with anger or unkindness may be hard to break, but our determination to express an empowering flow of love will lead us, with practice, to express greater and more consistent kindness with our love-mate.

This commitment on the part of both love-partners enormously strengthens the bond of love.

In my own meditation, I sometimes draw a circle on a sheet of paper and think of this as a barrel representing my consciousness. I then write down in the circle, with great honesty, what is in my consciousness – the good and the negative. Then I pray for the thoughts and insights that will remove the destructive elements from the circle of my thinking.

As I let my prayers remove what I know doesn't belong in this circle (my consciousness), I wait for an inner conviction that my barrel is full of only the qualities and substance of love.

Some of these negative thoughts have a persistent way of sneaking back in to the barrel of my consciousness, but I keep pushing them out.

Such prayer, meditation, or Love-cleansing enables us to bring to our day – and our love-mate – the full force of kindness + honesty.

Kindness + honesty
treasured and stored in consciousness
create an inevitable flow of
perfect love

Kindness + Honesty
in action

Here are *actions* that you can take right now to bring kindness + honesty into your love-life:

1. **Make a clear decision** in your own mind to be kind and honest to your love-mate and to become an expert using this power.

2. **Ask yourself**: How can I express more kindness + honesty to my love-mate?

3. **Practice being kind + honest right now** to your love-mate. Initiate a conversation with this motive in mind.

4. **Ask your love-mate**: *"What are you thinking, honey?"* Listen and respond with all the combined kindness + honesty you can generate.

5. **Respond with kindness + honesty**. Whenever your love-mate asks you: *"What are you thinking, honey?"* use this as an opportunity to practice being honest + kind.

6. **Maintain a flow of kindness + honesty** in your love-life. See if you can last one hour! One day! Better yet, commit to a life-time and you'll be leaping into the arms of perfect love.

7. **Wait! Think!** When a testy moment surfaces with your love-mate, think: *"Right at this second is an opportunity for me to practice honesty + kindness."* Do it! Give yourself the satisfaction and self-empowerment of rising above stress, anger, bad news, fear, doubt, or tension.

8. **Communicate your feelings**. If you feel your love-mate is not being kind + honest with you, communicate your feelings to your love-mate practicing kindness + honesty yourself. For example, you might say:

   "Sweetie, I'd like to discuss something that's important to me. I'd like us to feel closer to each other. Can we discuss this so both of us can feel more loved?"

9. **Give this book to your love-mate.** If you want your love-mate to have a greater understanding of the value of kindness + honesty, give this book with the thought:

   "Honey, this is a book that has been very helpful to me. I'd appreciate your reading it so you will know what is in my heart. I think this book will help us strengthen our love for each other."

10. **Surround yourself with friends** who treat you with kindness + honesty. Don't let yourself get cut off from a world waiting to support and love you.

11. **Affirm to yourself** that kindness and honesty are your spiritual right. Affirm:

*"I am worthy of being treated
with kindness + honesty
because I am Love's own expression
This is my innate right!
I will honor Love
by expressing kindness + honesty myself
and I will also honor Love
by acknowledging
my right
to be loved
with kindness + honesty
by my love-mate"*

Self-quiz

Kindness + Honesty

Directions: Rate yourself based on your relationship with
your love-mate. If you don't have a love-mate at this time,
circle where you want to be when you do have one.

1.   I am consistently kind to my love-mate:

  1   2   3   4   5   6   7   8   9   10

Not at all   Moderately   100%

2.   My love-mate is consistently kind to me:

  1   2   3   4   5   6   7   8   9   10

Not at all   Moderately   100%

3.   I am consistently honest with my love-mate:

  1   2   3   4   5   6   7   8   9   10

Not at all   Moderately   100%

4.   My love-mate is consistently honest with me:

  1   2   3   4   5   6   7   8   9   10

Not at all   Moderately   100%

5.   I feel emotionally safe and secure to share
      feelings openly with my love-mate:

  1   2   3   4   5   6   7   8   9   10

Not at all   Moderately   100%

6. My love-mate feels emotionally safe and secure to share feelings openly with me:

1   2   3   4   5   6   7   8   9   10
Not at all   Moderately   100%

7. I am in close touch with what my love-mate is thinking:

1   2   3   4   5   6   7   8   9   10
Not at all   Moderately   100%

8. My love-mate is in close touch with what I am thinking:

1   2   3   4   5   6   7   8   9   10
Not at all   Moderately   100%

9. I take time each day to quietly fill up with kindness + honesty so these will come out when I'm with my love-mate:

1   2   3   4   5   6   7   8   9   10
Not at all   Moderately   100%

10. My love-mate takes time each day to quietly fill up with kindness + honesty so these will come out in our life together:

1   2   3   4   5   6   7   8   9   10
Not at all   Moderately   100%

Self-rating
Kindness + Honesty

Total Score: _____ divided by 10= _____

1-2   Kindness + honesty vacuum. Time for radical revision or new possibilities.

3-4   Minimum kindness + honesty. Time to set higher standards.

5-6   Survivable kindness + honesty. Is this acceptable to you for the rest of your life?

7-8   Decent kindness + honesty. Why not go for the gold? What would make this a 10?

9-10   Living in the embrace of kindness + honesty. Rejoice!

Chapter 4

Cherishing
each other's dreams

Our dreams power the universe.

Within each of us are vast, creative dreams. We dream of what we would like to do, accomplish, and be.

For most of us, these dreams lay buried within the secrets of our inner soul. Our dreams are sometimes so fragile that we are too embarrassed to reveal them – sometimes even to ourselves.

It feels frightening to reveal them to those around us. What would they think? Crazy, egotistical, stupid – from another planet? Who are we to have such dreams?

Yet these dreams persist in our private consciousness.

*Each of us
is like a gem
at the bottom of the ocean –
hidden
by layers of
timidity and accepted limitations*

This is where perfect love rises to the zenith of liberation.

Perfect love
liberates
our dreams

Many of our secret dreams are squashed or imprisoned by how we are treated by others – and by our love-mate.

Nothing liberates the inner core of who we are as much as a love-mate who cherishes our dreams and loves us so deeply that our richest, deepest identity is brought to the surface, recognized, and gloriously valued.

My own dreams
liberated

I will never forget Shannon's liberation of my own private dreams.

Sitting in front of the fireplace at her home, in the first winter of our love, I felt her joy and the power of her caring. She asked me what I most desired in life.

In an instant, I silently reviewed my whole life – my hopes, dreams, failures, accomplishments, discouragements, present circumstances, choices, and possibilities – and came to a mental standstill. I felt I no longer knew what I truly desired. I was too discouraged to answer. I had no happy answer within me to give her.

Right then, Shannon declared:

> *"Let's affirm right now that you can know your highest purpose in life and that nothing can prevent that idea from coming forth in full completeness and visibility."*

Wow! I was not accustomed to such a powerful and loving affirmation.

Later that evening, still feeling Shannon's cherishing of my invisible dreams, something clicked so clearly in my private consciousness that I jumped for a pad of paper.

I felt so appreciated, so valued, so loved by Shannon that my fears, shame, confusion, inadequacies, challenges, and doubts vanished in my consciousness. Her listening and non-judgmental love called forth my true identity and caused a paradigm-shift in my sense of who I was. I felt the real me awakening. My dreams poured forth and were a revelation – even to me!

> *"I feel compelled to write a book that will open people to the love they deserve. I envision seven new rights advancing in consciousness as we enter the 21st century and I want to share them with the universe."*

To my own amazement, these seven rights spilled out on my yellow pad with what seemed to be 100% clarity to my inner senses.

I felt like a completely new person. Something deep within my consciousness had come to the surface. I felt that my lifepath had surfaced with great clarity.

Today, you are holding in your hands the book that is the first fruit of Shannon's cherishing of my dreams. Can you imagine how loved I felt?

Yes,

your love-mate

does have dreams!

Don't think for one second that your love-mate doesn't have dreams.

Each of us is full of great richness.

Any time you think this is not true of someone, take an hour with that person, forget yourself completely, and immerse yourself in listening actively to that person's heart and dreams. You will experience a fountain of creativity pour forth from the very soul of that person and you will have met a dear new friend. This is a powerful exercise.

Your love-mate may claim to have no dreams, but don't believe it.

I remember one experience in my life that remains with me as if it occurred today. I was a counselor at an adult education center for disadvantaged adults in New York. A young woman had applied to our center and I met with her during the enrollment process. I asked her, with great interest and compassion, what she wanted to accomplish in her life.

She looked at me, sensed my honest caring for her, even though we had just met, and began crying.

She cried for some time.

I gently asked her why she was crying and she said:

"You are the first person in my life
that has asked me that question."

She then spilled out her dreams, feeling embarrassed to even have them, not sure she was worthy to dream. I cherished her dreams with her and encouraged her. She had taken a step much higher than simply enrolling in a class.

An environment of genuine love, kindness, gentleness, caring, and patience allows dreams to surface

This is the environment that perfect love seeks to create for *each* love-mate. There is great caring, gentleness, and patience as we cherish the dreams that we *know* are there. We are internally committed to the revealing of our love-mate's dreams, and nothing throws us off-course, even a love-mate that insists, *"I have no dreams!"*

If you or your love-mate think you have no dreams, this is your golden moment to relax in your love-mate's cherishing and let your dreams surface in your consciousness.

♦ Perhaps you were never allowed to dream.

♦ Perhaps you were called stupid.

♦ Perhaps you have been considered subordinate.

♦ Perhaps you consider yourself to be inadequate.

♦ Perhaps, perhaps, perhaps...

Perfect love dismantles all these roadblocks, takes away the mental chains that bind us from feeling free to dream, to aspire, to be, to listen to our innermost desires.

Start asking probing questions – with great love – and you'll discover a gift of Soul in your midst.

It doesn't matter if your love-mate's dreams come forth awkwardly or vaguely.

♦ Practice your listening skills (chapter 6, *Listening to the heart*) and *be quiet!*

♦ Provide an environment of caring, tenderness, freedom, and patience, and your love-mate's dreams will focus into elegant beauty.

Do you see the bigger event taking place as you cherish your love-mate's dreams?

It is even more than your love-mate's dreams coming to the surface. It is even more than your love-mate feeling a great sense of joy and liberation in feeling the power of these internal dreams.

The bigger event is that your relationship with your love-mate is being transformed to a vastly higher level of love.

***When our love-mate
cherishes our dreams,
we feel the
divine presence of
Love itself***

Your

dreams

are just as important

Don't ever believe that it is your role to provide an environment for your love-mate's dreams to surface, but that it is not equally your right to experience your dreams coming forth.

In most love-relationships, one member is often subordinate. This is a love travesty.

In perfect love, such a consciousness is unthinkable!

*It is your
right
to have your dreams
cherished, supported,
and
honored*

Feel your love-mate's dreams as a vital part of *your* happiness

As you listen to your love-mate's dreams, take an even higher step than listening.

Relish – as part of *your* happiness – these dreams. Incorporate your love-mate's dreams into your own unfolding life.

What if your love-mate's dreams do not interest you? This is not unnatural for many relationships. Unfortunately, these love-mates grow, develop, and achieve in separate, unknown worlds to each other.

In perfect love, our love-mate's dreams and ambitions are so important to us that we get involved in thinking about them too – and this involvement wakens us to their value.

Here's an example with my own love-mate.

Shannon is so satisfied in her full-time occupation as a Christian Science practitioner (a spiritual healer) that when I listen to her and cherish her dreams, her love of healing spills out like an ocean overflowing with joy. And I find myself valuing even more deeply what she is doing.

This valuing doesn't mean that I have to do the same thing as Shannon. But it does mean that I feel connected to her heart, to her dreams – to her life purpose. And she feels the enormous bond of love this connection creates.

One day, I wanted to be sure I was in touch with Shannon's inner heart so I asked her if she had any other dreams.

"No," she said, but then rather tentatively added, *"except maybe to learn how to paint well."*

I leaped in with enthusiasm, encouragement, and ideas for expressing this, but I could see her instantly backing off.

I saw immediately that I had made a big mistake. Rather than listening to her, letting *her* thoughts remain the focus, I had interjected my own enthusiasm and *I* was running forward with *her* dreams.

I have learned to more quietly listen as Shannon cherishes and shares her desires with me.

Today, as I am writing this chapter, Shannon is painting away in an art class she takes once a week with a teacher she greatly admires.

It doesn't matter to me whether she paints (although I love her work). What matters to me is that she has the freedom to explore all that she wants to be – with my complete encouragement and cherishing.

The results
of my dreams cherished

Here's a potent example of what happens when dreams are cherished.

When I came back from my three-week photo-trip to Central Asia, I had taken over 2,000 pictures.

Some of them were beautiful – like this woman in Turkmenistan celebrating the first anniversary of her country's independence from the Soviet Union.

Although I was a competent photographer, I was only beginning to feel like an artist.

Something within me yearned to take truly beautiful photographs – to express more soulfully what I felt inside.

Shannon listened so lovingly and encouragingly to this song within my heart that I felt it was legitimate to dream of reaching this capacity.

Her cherishing and nurturing of my dreams led me to attend several weekend photo-workshops that I never would have attended without my dreams receiving such tender support.

These workshops transformed my photographic skills. I learned more in three days than I had learned in the past 20 years. I learned so much, not just because the workshops were effective, but because I felt the power of Shannon's enormous support and love for all I wanted to be. I felt such unconditional caring and support that I was able to relax into my own being, sink into the inviting world around me, and immerse myself with my camera into the beauty I felt – without fear, guilt, or doubt.

The most unexpected outcome took place.

I ended up with so many delightful images, that I started making and selling note cards with original photos on the front. And then I began adding messages to the backs of these cards – expressing poetically and metaphysically what the image meant to me.

Well, composing these messages launched the book you are now holding. This book, which before seemed impossible to write for lack of time, confidence, and a million other reasons, started spilling out!

I couldn't stop writing. The song within me poured out of my consciousness faster than I could write – all triggered by Shannon's cherishing of my dreams.

How could I possibly feel more loved!

This is the cherishing of inner dreams that we each deserve.

Tenacity

***Nothing
can stop
the unfolding
of
who we are
and
what we cherish***

Chapter 5

Genuine Equality

Genuine equality
will
transform
your love life

Throughout planet Earth, the vast majority of men and women are either unconscious or barely-conscious of genuine equality.

This sad reality is a tragedy of immense proportion and affects every love-relationship on our planet. Equality in our love-relationships is grossly overlooked.

A profound revolution is at work, however, trembling and shaking loose our vast denial and ignorance of genuine equality. This revolution will alter the path of civilization – and our love-lives. Let us bring to the forefront of consciousness what genuine equality means in our love lives.

Genuine equality means that deep within our private consciousness, we cherish, demand, and create the opportunity for our love-mate to experience the same depth of joy, opportunity, and quality of love that we expect and cherish for ourselves.

Genuine equality is bold, clear, unequivocal. It tells us:

> *"I am honored, treasured, equally important, and equally free to be all that I dream. I am never subordinate to my love-mate, and my love-mate is never subordinate to me – in any circumstance."*

As we enter Millennium consciousness, we are being called forth to understand, accept, and experience the full reality of genuine equality in our love lives. It is your right, whether you are a woman or a man, to experience equality in every facet of your relationship with your love-mate:

♦ in the way your identity is perceived.
♦ in love-making.
♦ in lifepath fulfillment.
♦ in finances.
♦ in socializing.
♦ in daily living.

**Genuine equality
is an
inherent, essential,
indisputable, non-negotiable
right
in our love lives**

Let's look at genuine equality more closely.

Genuine equality
in the way
your identity is perceived

Nothing is more fundamental to the fabric of our identity than the way we are perceived by others.

At this core level of identity, there remains deep and terrible injustice throughout the world when comparing women and men.

A woman's substance – worth – is still too often measured as physical by men. A man's worth is more likely to be measured by what he has accomplished.

Although laws have been passed to end discrimination in the workplace, laws cannot penetrate to the inner consciousness that fails to grasp the necessity of genuine, felt-in-the-heart equality.

How genuine can equality be when women are still so widely (even though more quietly) evaluated for their bodies, while men are more often evaluated on their overall achievements?

For men reading this book, suppose that every time you walked into work or a social gathering, you were *primarily* evaluated on how your body looked rather than your unique talents and accomplishments. Would this be satisfying?

Of course not! Yet this is the demeaning atmosphere of thought surrounding most women's lives – and it has devastating consequences to a love relationship.

If a man is thinking
that a woman's body is her primary substance,
he cannot help
expressing and communicating this
even if no words are spoken

It's as if a man were saying out loud:

"I see you primarily as a body which
looks beautiful and sexy -- or a body
that doesn't appeal to me."

This attitude is equally debilitating when expressed by a woman towards a man. If he is primarily identified by his physical appeal, his true substance is missed.

In either case, these relationships play out on the most superficial level. A relationship built on physical attraction alone is a setup for vast disappointment.

A relationship focused
primarily
on physical attraction
is highly unlikely
to include genuine equality

Why? Because a relationship centered foremost on physical attraction puts such high priority on physical appeal that the concept of equality – not to mention genuine equality – is not likely to appear on the mental landscape of top love ingredients.

Genuine equality just won't happen unless it's way up there on the love-list – in your mind and your love-mate's.

Of course we are physically attracted to our love-mates! This is natural and wonderful. But in perfect love, the inner substance of our love-mate is honored above all else.

Here's what takes place in the love you deserve:

◆ Love-mates look at each other as complete equals and cherish that equality. They seek to love each other in exactly the way they would like to be loved themselves.

◆ Love-mates recognize that the real substance of this equality is not physical. It is the cherishing of qualities, talents, desires, dreams, goals, and life-purpose.

We cannot have rich, satisfying love without genuine equality

This is the revolution taking place in our love lives. The call for you to be treated with genuine equality by your love-mate – and for you to treat your love-mate with genuine equality – may seem startling, but only because it is so missing in our love lives.

We have a long way to go to experience this consciousness of perfect love, but this mental step must be taken to liberate our love lives.

Claiming your right to genuine equality is the single most significant step you can take towards experiencing perfect love

Envisioning
genuine equality

Envision a relationship of perfect love with genuine equality at its core. If we could look into the internal consciousness of a man or woman experiencing genuine equality in their relationship, what would we see?

We would see each love-mate cherishing the other, supporting the other, listening to the other, going to great lengths to ensure that the other was deeply satisfied – in lovemaking, in reaching life dreams, in decision-making, in finances – in every nook of their lives together.

We would see each love-mate protecting, defending, promoting, and remembering each other's innate goodness, even during stressful moments – never losing sight of the other's glorious identity.

◆

If we could capture a man's private thoughts, we might hear him thinking to himself:

"I love this woman.

I want her to experience every single pleasure that I experience. I want her to feel esteemed as an equal in our relationship. I want her to experience true equality in our relationship – in our lovemaking, decision-making, reaching for inner dreams, handling of finances, socializing, and in our daily living together.

If I find that I am not treating her this way, I want that revealed. I do not want her to feel a hidden, inner sense of subordination. I do not want generations of masculine domination to obstruct my love-mate from experiencing the power of genuine equality. And I do not want generations of feminine subordination to debilitate her awareness or ability to step into her right to genuine equality.

I look forward to loving her in a tender, rich way and having her experience true equality. I look forward to a continuing love-exploration with her that will raise us up together in the consciousness and power of equality.

I want to know what she most cherishes in life, what she wants to accomplish, how she honestly feels as we love each other, what she is thinking at her deepest level.

Even as I cherish this equality for her, I equally cherish this right for myself. I will not allow myself to be treated with any less equality than that which I treasure for her. I am inwardly committed to a relationship that blesses each of us to the maximum, and I know that genuine equality is non-negotiable for this to happen."

If you are a woman, think of the above as the inner voice of the lover you deserve

If you are a man, compare this to your present consciousness as you think of your love-mate.

♦

If we could capture a woman's private thoughts, we might hear her thinking:

"I love this man.

I have a vast depth of love to share with him, and I want him to feel all of it. I want him to reach for his highest dreams.

I am going to love him with every ounce of my being. I want him to feel unburdened, supported, cherished, and happy.

I want to love him so thoroughly that he realizes that he doesn't have to perform in order to be loved. I want to see his great qualities and name them to him so he can see how I admire and love him.

I want to encourage him to grow as much as he wants to and applaud this growth. I want to hold his hand, comfort his fears, understand his heart, and help him realize his dreams.

I want him to know how wonderful he is to the world and how much he means to me, and never take him for granted.

As much as I want all this for him, I also want all this from him – for myself. I want us each to feel the bliss of loving each other with full equality."

**If you
are a man,
think of the above
as the inner voice of
the lover you deserve**

If you are a woman, compare this to your consciousness as you think of your love-mate.

◆

How much of these dialogues are real in *your* private heart?

Genuine equality
in lovemaking

Love-making unmistakably reveals the presence
– or absence – of genuine equality.

♦ Whose desires and needs are most
important?

♦ Are both love-mates equally open and
honest?

♦ Do both feel equally honored?

Without genuine equality, lovemaking is full of
power, performance, dominance, submission, even
faked "satisfaction." Deep-down, no one is truly
satisfied.

In perfect love, there is a keen awareness that
both partners deserve to experience the fullness of
love.

Envision the liberation that would occur if men
in lovemaking were not focused on performing, but
could enjoy the experience of being truly sensitive to
their love-mate, and relax in their love-making?

In perfect love, there is tender, honest
communication of each other's desires and this
consciousness is devoid of power, dominance, or
performance concerns. It is a consciousness that
esteems and feels esteemed. No one loses.

Orgasm is not the goal. Experiencing each other
at the most intimate level of tenderness, unity,
honoring, and esteem is the ecstasy. This depth of
intimacy is unachievable without genuine equality.

Men and women experience satisfaction in
different ways, and both partners in perfect love take
great joy in meeting each other's needs equally. Is

she being encouraged to tell him what gives her the most pleasure? Is he?

There is great vulnerability in lovemaking. Past treatment, abuse, inability, self-doubt, and lack of trust are powerful negative forces.

It is precisely in these most sensitive moments that perfect love is experienced and treasured!

It is a consciousness that seeks to help each partner feel deeply loved, not just physically, but emotionally. This often calls forth our most needed moments of listening, cherishing, and respecting each other's needs.

Here is the potent question:

After love-making,
do you feel
cherished, honored, esteemed,
empowered?

Genuine equality
in lifepath fulfillment

Genuine equality
liberates
our creativity

In perfect love, each love-mate's dreams are equally cherished.

It has traditionally been the woman's role to provide emotional and moral support to a man and his occupation. Today, with more relationships where both men and women are working, this stereotype is fading, but it is still present. The man's job is still more likely to be considered an "occupation" and a step along a significant lifepath where a woman's job is often considered more temporary, and not a part of a significant lifepath.

There are natural reasons for this, of course. For one, women often interrupt or stop their careers to have children. Yet, regardless of circumstances, the real issue beneath the surface is whether the woman's lifepath goals are valued equally.

Perhaps her choice in life (or his) is to be a full-time homemaker and child-raiser, at least for a few years. Just think of the incredible importance of this choice. Is there a higher lifepath pursuit than raising a child in an environment of love, morals, and a sense of worth? Wouldn't this be an immense contribution toward furthering peace, eliminating crime, and establishing a better world? A love-mate taking on such an awesome task deserves honor, support, nurturing, and empowerment.

In perfect love, there is a deep desire to enable each love-mate to identify and reach for lifepath dreams. There is an understanding that *lifepath* is a broader, more meaningful concern than *occupation* and defines our life purpose and the highest use of our talents.

If the choice is made to have children, this does not dilute the importance of the woman's lifepath goals.

What are her dreams?

What are his?

These are treasured questions in perfect love, and the answer by each partner is equally treasured.

♦ Both partners see each other's occupational and lifepath goals as equally valid and important.

♦ Both love-mates are keenly sensitive to each other's life-dreams. They listen to each other repeatedly. They probe to understand, to bring out. They cherish.

Genuine equality
in finances

Money is power.

Inequality on the money front means inequality on the power front.

In perfect love, such inequality is unacceptable.

Inequality with finances within a love-relationship has disastrous consequences for women:

- ◆ It is a tragedy to countless women that, after entering into a love partnership, they do not know how much actual money exists in their partnership, where it is, where the complete records are kept, and how to track and manage this money themselves. They are often left out when financial decisions are made.

- ◆ It is also a tragedy that too many husbands leave their wives for another woman – and often at a point when reaching financial success. These wives often don't know how much money exists beyond the household checking account. Small wonder that women suffer so much more financially in a divorce than men.

- ◆ It is likewise devastating that many widowed women, who did not participate equally in financial decision-making with their husbands, are exposed to great abuse by those who profit by their unempowered ignorance.

Each instance of such inequality with finances tells a woman that she is not equal and not respected – in knowledge, intelligence, capacity, or worth. It undermines trust.

Would a man tolerate this with his business partner? Of course not! Why should a love partner put up with such inequality?

Inequality with finances also has terrible consequences for men:

♦ The tragedy for men is that the practice of not being open with finances unempowers their love-mate. Does such a man honestly expect to be richly loved by someone he has stripped of equality? How much love can flow from this condition? How much love is the man sacrificing? A ton!

♦ The inner loss for men who treat their love-mates with financial inequality is even worse. Many men live their entire productive work lives in quiet, nervous desperation, hoping to produce enough income for the family. The deep, inbred belief that it is a man's responsibility to "bring home the bacon" creates enormous guilt and burden.

A relationship cannot exist at the level of perfect love with such inequality.

Financial equality
empowers
our love relationship

Women today are in the workforce just as substantially as men. A two-income relationship is the norm. In fact, in dual-income families, 22% of women out-earn their husbands, according to a 1997 report by the United States Bureau of Labor Statistics.

But what do we find when we dig into how finances are handled? In too many cases, the partners have not addressed and challenged the powerful traditions that have preceded their relationship. There is still residual thinking that finances are the man's area of expertise, even though this attitude is diminishing.

In perfect love, this old paradigm of consciousness is completely thrown out. There is a deep commitment – by both partners – to empower each other as equals, and this is felt at all levels of financial management of their assets.

It is not a question of each doing an equal part of each task, but a recognition that if each of them understands what is going on with the money, they will both be genuinely empowered and come to mutual, well-discussed decisions together.

This attitude shifts any burden of financial responsibility from his shoulders alone (or hers, if the roles are reversed) to the more powerful shoulders of the partnership. This equal sharing of the burden resolves these needs into joint choices that empower both partners.

It can also be deeply empowering when the love-mate that is not the principal income earner is given the opportunity to manage and track the finances. The benefit of this is enormous in perfect love. The love-mate not working, or who is bringing in the minority share of income, is empowered by full disclosure of financial information, participation in management, and the learning of valuable skills.

The other love-mate is equally empowered by no longer being the only one who truly knows their financial condition – no longer having to carry the burden of financial juggling or decision-making alone.

In perfect love, both love-mates have open discussions to decide budget issues, options, priorities, and financial strategies. They act as a support and comfort to each other, lightening each other's load.

Perfect love includes a commitment and joy in full financial disclosure, completely open financial records, and great sensitivity to not overspending without mutual consent.

Each partner wants the other to experience genuine financial equality and sees financial dealings as another way to demonstrate their great love for each other.

Genuine equality
in socializing

Socializing with others is another arena of life where genuine equality is deeply honored.

When you are in a social setting with other love partners, how long does it take to determine whether two people love each other with equality?

About three seconds. The evidence of inequality is instantly obvious:

♦ How often does one partner put down the other, either openly, or with subtle looks and behaviors?

♦ Is a woman judged by her substance or her looks? Is a man?

♦ Are each love-mate's thoughts on issues solicited – and valued – equally?

♦ Is each partner aware when the other partner is being put down by another?

♦ Does a love-mate intercede to ensure equality – or does the love-mate allow a humiliating or offensive remark to pass for social reasons?

In perfect love,
genuine equality
exists everywhere – all the time –
with your love-mate

In perfect love, there is alert sensitivity to valuing each partner's contribution and expression of ideas. And there is alert sensitivity to the way a love-partner is being treated by others.

For example, an offensive joke that puts down women is not ignored simply to be socially polite. Would we allow our children or our mothers to be put down? No! Is your love-mate less important?

Poor-taste or abuse in humor is graciously addressed rather than politely ignored. Why should "friends" be allowed to attack the very fabric of your love relationship – even indirectly?

The impact of inequality in social circles is demeaning and comes directly home with you and your love-mate once you leave the party.

Here's another example. Some love-mates show blatant interest in other women or men – right in front of their love-mates. This attitude, even if an unconscious or social habit, is utterly demeaning to a love-mate. Many love-partners let this slide by unchallenged because they are accustomed to abuse, even if mild. *"Oh that's just the way he (or she) is."*

It's time for this to cease.

Wake up men! Wake up women!

Here, again, is the potent test. Next time you are in a social gathering with your love-mate, stop at random and ask yourself privately:

Do I feel honored, valued, empowered?
Does my love-mate?

Genuine equality
in daily living

Genuine equality is an atmosphere – not something pulled out of hiding from time to time when your love-mate is unhappy.

Genuine equality doesn't stop and start. One knows genuine equality by its consistency. It's a cherishing that is pervasive in every aspect of your daily life with your love-mate. Real equality between love-mates is so genuine that it sneaks into the smallest portions of our daily lives.

Shannon and I laugh at ourselves in the way we almost compete for who will be first to drag out the garbage cans, bring in the groceries, clean up after a meal, or provide that small touch of love that brings a smile to the inner heart.

Envision multiplying this attitude to every task that confronts a loving couple. It is immensely empowering. It lubricates the foundation of the love relationship. It is as if you say to each other a thousand times each day:

> *"I love living with you. I want to make*
> *your life a joy! I want to ease your*
> *load as much as possible. I want us*
> *to relish living together."*

Genuine equality is not measured by whether each does half of each routine. Shannon does most of the cooking and shopping in our daily routine. I'm not completely comfortable with this, because a woman's traditional role of cooking is so often unappreciated, so I am sensitive to any signs that she would rather eat out or have me cook (the first being the more tasty option). We eat out a lot!

I am also sensitive to the fact that the person cooking can easily get the idea that he or she is subservient in the relationship. So I make sure that Shannon feels appreciated – because I am truly grateful for her taking on this task. I don't allow myself to sink into an attitude of expecting service.

Take another routine in a love relationship – driving. Both love-mates jump in the car to go somewhere, anywhere. Who's the driver? Was there a discussion? Does each get equal opportunity? Do you know your partner's preference?

Shannon and I both *love* to drive. When we first met, I recognized Shannon's love of driving (it wasn't hard – she was already at the wheel) and I cherished her opportunity to be in command in the traditionally male-dominated driver's seat.

As our love – and our equality – continued to unfold, we both realized that we were a bit off-balance on this front. So we tilted the balance towards equality. I now drive 30% of the time!

Each tiny moment of routine life adds up to an overwhelming sense of equality – or an overwhelming sense of inequality.

- Who drives?
- Who gets the most comfortable chair?
- Who decides which movie to see?
- Who decides what car to buy?
- Who takes out the garbage?
- Who cleans up?
- Who controls the remote control?

There is nothing routine
in perfect love
nothing too small
to be valued through the lens of equality

Are you experiencing genuine equality?

Without genuine equality, perfect love cannot exist! But *with* genuine equality, your love-relationship will rise to heights never before envisioned.

It is vital that you claim your *right* to experience genuine equality in your love-life.

As you answer the questions on the next page, don't panic if your scores are not high. Use these questions to:

♦ Honor the strengths in your love-relationship and identify the weaknesses.

♦ Establish a standard for genuine equality in your love-life.

The power of equality
is so
potent
that it alone
can almost fuel
perfect love

Self-quiz
Genuine equality

Directions: Rate yourself on your relationship with your love-mate. If you don't have a love-mate at this time, circle where you want to be when you do.

1. I experience genuine equality in love-making:

    1   2   3   4   5   6   7   8   9   10

    Not at all   To some degree   Completely

2. My life dreams are cherished and supported equally with my love-mate's life dreams:

    1   2   3   4   5   6   7   8   9   10

    Not at all   To some degree   Completely

3. I am treated with equality in finances:

    1   2   3   4   5   6   7   8   9   10

    Not at all   To some degree   Completely

4. I am treated with equality by my love-mate in social gatherings:

    1   2   3   4   5   6   7   8   9   10

    Not at all   To some degree   Completely

5. I am treated with equality in the routine of our daily life together:

    1   2   3   4   5   6   7   8   9   10

    Not at all   To some degree   Completely

Self-Rating
Genuine equality

Total Score: _____ divided by 5 = _____

1-2   Equality vacuum. Time for radical revision or new possibilities.

3-4   Minimal equality. Time to set higher standards.

5-6   Survivable equality. Is this acceptable to you for the rest of your life?

7-8   Decent equality. Why not go for the gold? What would move you to a 10?

9-10   Genuine equality. Rejoice!

Chapter 6

Listening
to the heart

Has anyone ever listened to you?

I mean, listened with such focused attention and reverence for what is in your inner heart that you felt completely understood?

Most of us, unfortunately, are rarely listened to at this depth – by anyone, including our love-mates.

The power of true listening is awesome.

♦ It opens mental and emotional doors.

♦ It tells us we are loved.

♦ It enables us to know ourselves.

♦ It opens our lives to revelation.

♦ It creates enormous intimacy.

♦ It bonds us together.

♦ It satisfies our heart and soul.

♦ We feel loved.

Yet so few people listen. So few know *how* to listen. What a loss!

There is no greater gift than to listen to your love-mate's heart

How many people in your entire life have listened to your heart?

Go ahead, count them.

How many people can you name who know what is truly unfolding in your private consciousness *right now*?

Does your love-mate?

Do you even know what it feels like to be truly listened to?

Let's find out right now.

What's going on
in your heart
right now?

Allow me the privilege of listening to you – right now.

Even though I am not physically present with you, I am a real person speaking to you. And I am a good listener. So imagine that I am with you now.

Slow down your reading for a moment and silently ask yourself:

> *What is honestly going on in my heart right now? What am I quietly thinking within my deepest, private consciousness about my life at this moment?*

◆

As you prepare to share with me whatever you wish to share, I am looking at you with great caring.

I am offering you complete and quiet space to think and share without interruption.

I am listening with love and interest. There is no hurry to answer. There is no judgment.

◆

I genuinely want to know what is going on in your heart. In my verbal silence, I hope that my eyes are showing you how much I care. I honor you.

I want you to feel the freedom to unpack whatever concerns, desires, or doubts you wish to share. Go ahead. Speak to me silently or out loud.

◆

As you begin to speak, gathering thoughts, I am tempted to say something – to make you feel more comfortable, to get you started, to agree with you, or to add my feelings or thoughts to what you have said – but, no, I resist.

Instead, I stay in the mode of active but very quiet listening – in attentive, loving silence – allowing you the freedom to continue unfolding what is in your heart, even though it may be slow in coming out.

◆

As you slowly open to me (and yourself), surprised to find yourself with so much space to speak without interruption, judgment, or direction, I continue to relish this moment of listening to your heart. Your long pauses, however, test my listening skills.

Silence is awkward...

◆

...but oh so beautiful! In silence, the heart opens.

I have learned the skill of silence and I happily present this gift to you. Please continue unfolding what's in your heart.

◆

As you speak, I am tempted to let my private, internal thinking shift from you to *me* – to *my* life, *my* reaction to what you are saying, *my* conclusions, *my* expectations of what you will say next, and *my* judgments.

But I remind myself, internally, that true listening only takes place when I focus only on what *you* are saying, not on my reaction, judgment, or conclusions.

I return mentally to you.

◆

As I make the effort to successfully stay tuned to your heart, not mine, I find myself feeling more and more at one with you.

I am beginning to truly understand you. It is an extraordinary experience to listen so openly and non-judgmentally.

◆

As I continue listening to you without the distortion or noise of my own life, I begin to discover the depth of what is truly taking place in your heart.

I am in awe. You, too, are in awe, almost disbelieving this enormous space of freedom to let your heart come forward. Do you have more to share?

◆

My continued silence opens the door for you to share more. Your heart is beginning to appear with increasing clarity. You come to a stopping point.

♦ Is it really the end?
♦ Should I break this unbelievably long and silent listening?
♦ Are you getting annoyed at too much listening with no feedback?

I think these questions privately, and communicate to you with my eyes and heart that I want you to feel the space to do what your heart delights. I do not want to interrupt your inner flow. This may be a pause of self-discovery. You may have more to say.

I will not let myself break the silence that allows you the freedom to continue without diversion. If there is more within you that needs to come forth, I want you to have the experience of all that is within you being cherished.

♦

The silence between us is sacred. I see you searching your heart at even greater depth. My highest love at this precious and profound moment is continued quietness.

You continue speaking. I am listening with unconditional acceptance. I want to understand, not judge. You are almost unaware of me now, continuing to explore and speak at even greater depth. Inwardly, you are surprised that anyone has listened to you so thoroughly – allowed you so much space to unfold.

You reach another end point. I sense that you have had the opportunity to say all you wish to share for now. I see your satisfaction in getting so much of your heart out in the open. I see the dawning of your realization:

> *"So this is what it feels like when someone truly listens to your heart!"*

◆

Thank you for opening to me. I know now – with vastly more depth – what is going on within you. We both do! We have connected.

Real listening
says to our love-mate:
"I cherish what is in your heart"

I truly wish I could sit with each reader of this book who has never experienced such listening. But now you know what you deserve.

Each of us needs the satisfaction – the healing – that pours forth during such listening.

- ◆ When was the last time anyone listened to you with such tenderness, quietness, thoroughness, and genuine interest?
- ◆ When was the last time your love-mate listened to your heart in such a way that you felt satisfied in sharing all that was within your heart?
- ◆ When was the last time you listened to your love-mate (or anyone) with this quality of honoring, liberating listening?

To feel
understood in your inner heart
is to experience
the love you deserve

The secrets of
listening

The secrets of listening are simple to understand – but little practiced.

When others listen to our heart with love:

- ♦ They are quiet.
- ♦ They don't interrupt.
- ♦ They don't lead us.
- ♦ They don't interject.
- ♦ They don't judge.
- ♦ They are experts at empathy.

They listen ever so quietly – with such a great desire to understand us that we can feel this caring.

When we pause to ponder our own thoughts, they don't break the silence. They listen even to our silence, telling us without words that what we are saying is valuable. They quietly support us in getting it all out.

We don't feel judged – because we are not being judged! When we think we have finished speaking, we pause, but there is no interruption.

We feel free to speak – unfold – even in silence or awkward attempts until it is clear that our heart has spoken openly and completely. We feel loved by the genuine focus that seeks to know and cherish what is in our heart.

Most of us seldom experience anyone listening to us this way. Next time you are with friends, or with your love-mate, mentally think about what is taking place in the communication with you. Ask yourself:

♦ Does anyone care about what's in my heart?

♦ Is anyone listening to my heart?

In a relationship based on perfect love, both love-mates yearn to understand each other's hearts, not just during courtship, but forever. This is a continual commitment.

How fast does it take for your love-mate to be out-of-touch with your feelings, ideas, dreams, and plans?

Minutes, not days!

It is astounding how fast our internal thoughts of life – our feelings, ideas, desires, plans – change.

If you listened to your love-mate yesterday, that's little guarantee that you are still in touch with his or her heart today.

Underneath all this discussion of listening, there is one skill that outshines them all for staying in tune with your love-mate's heart – the skill of empathy.

Becoming an expert
at empathy

To become an expert listener, you have no choice but to become an expert at empathy.

> **E**mpathy means that you listen so thoroughly and non-judgmentally, that you really do understand your love-mate's words and feelings, *and* your love-mate also feels your genuine understanding.

There are many "appearances" of listening, but empathy is the real thing. For example:

- ♦ We can listen – and have no idea of what someone just said.
- ♦ We can listen intently to someone's words – but have no idea what they mean.
- ♦ We can listen – while we inwardly respond in anger, disgust, jealousy, or judgment.
- ♦ We can listen – while we are quietly engrossed in preparing our response.

None of these qualify as real listening. To put it another way, how would you feel if someone listened to you in any of these ways? Not well honored! And certainly not well understood.

There are many kinds of listening and it would be unproductive and frustrating to always listen intently to your love-mate without speaking out yourself. Most conversations are give and take sharings.

There are times, however, when our hearts yearn to sing and be heard. These are the times where empathy unlocks your love-mate's heart and conveys pure, liberating love.

Empathy
with
genuine caring
is the key
that
unlocks the heart

Here are five steps to becoming an expert empathizer. These steps will enable you to connect with your love-mate at a much deeper level.

Step 1

Decide to listen

This is a giant decision.

It means that you decisively enter your love-mate's world and leave your own world of thoughts, needs, activities, and planning for the time being.

There is no half-way position. You either tune-in to your love-mate or you miss the boat. Most people miss the boat.

Why? Because most of us are so engrossed in our own thoughts, needs, interests, priorities, and feelings that we rarely make this leap into another's heart.

It takes great unselfishness and genuine caring to make this transition. But when you do, this is the leap that transforms a relationship.

If you think this is easy, try listening to someone right now with full empathy. Check how quickly you are sidetracked by your own internal thoughts.

Step 2

Tune-in

non-verbally

Listen to your love-mate with your mind and body – not with your mouth.

Tune-in non-verbally to your love-mate and show your interest and respect and love through direct, encouraging eye contact and body language.

Few people communicate with direct eye contact. You might be surprised how difficult it is to look your love-mate directly in the eyes.

***Direct eye contact
shows a desire to be intimate,
to be at one with your love-mate,
to understand***

Try this experiment. The next time someone is supposedly listening to you, check out their eyes and see how often they wander and glaze. You will begin to appreciate the power of body language.

It may seem subtle to you, but even a small shift of body and eye language tells your love-mate that you have wandered off mentally into your own world, no longer truly hearing.

Faking doesn't work.

Even if you think you are successful at faking good listening, your love-mate will have already sensed this lack of genuine connection and will have stopped communicating from the heart. You may still be hearing words, but it won't be from your love-mate's inner heart.

To put it another way, you can't fake real love.

♦ Do you really want to listen?

♦ Do you really care?

♦ Are you honestly prepared to tune-in?

These are the questions your eyes and body will answer.

Step 3

Listen

with

unconditional caring

What happens when you visit a good counselor or therapist? You are listened to with empathy and unconditional caring.

- ◆ The counselor listens with full body attention.
- ◆ The counselor listens without judgment.
- ◆ The counselor truly wants to understand you.
- ◆ The counselor cares for your well-being.
- ◆ You feel this love and slowly open your heart because of the environment of unconditional caring and non-judgment.

For many people, the only person who has ever truly listened to them is a counselor. Isn't this a shame?

Why should you and your love-mate be deprived of such powerful, liberating communication with each other?

As you let the ideas in this chapter sink into your consciousness, you will not only become an expert listener, but you will become an empowerer. You will discover the immense joy of empowering another person through real listening.

Let this central, powerful idea sink totally into your consciousness:

To listen to your love-mate
without judgment
is one of the
highest forms of love
you can give

Name the people in your life right now who *listen to you* with unconditional caring and no judgment.

♦ _____

♦ _____

♦ _____

♦ _____

♦ _____

Name the people in your life who *you listen to* with unconditional caring and no judgment.

♦ _____

♦ _____

♦ _____

♦ _____

♦ _____

You may have a very short list!

You can enlarge this list immediately by simply opening your heart to the desire to listen genuinely.

Here's what you can do right now:

Put this book down and go listen with unconditional caring and without judgment to your love-mate (or anyone).

Let your very being communicate the following
message:

> *"I want to treasure what's in your
> heart. I am actively listening to you –
> caring for you – right now, with no
> other motive than for you to feel
> understood and have the opportunity
> to share with me what is in your
> heart.*
>
> *I want you to feel the full freedom
> of communicating with me in an
> environment of total non-judgment.*
>
> *I want you to feel honored and
> accepted as you are."*

Step 4

Use the power

of silence

How do listeners most rapidly fall off the bridge of good listening? By opening their mouths – even when their intentions are admirable.

As soon as
you open your mouth
real listening
stops

Here's what happens:

Let's say you are intently listening to your love-mate and your love-mate is momentarily struggling for the right word or idea. If you make the mistake of trying to supply the missing word or idea, even if you're sure you know what it will be, you will immediately derail true listening.

Why? Because you have now forced your love-mate to think about *your* word. You have shifted the center of focus from your love-mate to you. Furthermore, your choice for the missing word will be wrong most of the time.

Likewise, when your love-mate says something that strikes a reaction within you, whether favorable or unfavorable, and you jump in to share *your* reaction, you will most probably derail your love-mate's heart.

Don't expect to say, "I'm sorry" and have your love-mate nimbly carry on. Your interruption will break the flow of your love-mate moving towards the center of his or her heart.

Why? Because, once again, you have shifted the focus to *you* and away from your love-mate. People just don't flow from the heart when there are interruptions.

When your love-partner comes to a pause and it's not clear whether he or she has more to say, or will continue, give your love-mate the silence that empowers. Here is where the temptation to jump in becomes enormous. Don't! Allow your love-mate the joy of experiencing the freedom to relax in patient silence, gather momentum, and go forward.

If you stay tuned to your love-mate's heart at exactly this awkward point, your love-mate, in the vast majority of cases, will continue launching forward and you will learn what you would have otherwise aborted.

Test this. You will be amazed at what you have been missing. And your love-mate will be amazed at how much more comes out in your presence.

Your love
expressed as silence
says
"I love you"
with liberating force

Step 5

Reflect back

what your love-mate is

saying and feeling

There is a valuable exception to remaining silent while listening. Without some proof from you, how does your love-mate know you are honestly and accurately tuned in?

In fact, how do *you* know?

The most powerful way to show your love-mate that you are tuned in is to reflect back, *occasionally*, what you are hearing. Here's how:

As your love-mate is sharing from the heart, ask yourself silently,

> *What is my love-mate truly saying and feeling? Can I identify it and convey it so accurately that my love-mate would say "Yes!" and continue flowing forward?"*

Don't put your love-mate's thoughts into your own words or interpretation. Try to reflect back the substance (not the literal words) of what you are hearing.

This is not easy, but it is extremely empowering.

For example, if your love-mate has been discussing goals and is obviously pleased with what is coming out, you might add quietly, during a pause:

> *"I can see you're feeling wonderful about your plans."*

Then listen quietly to your love-mate's response – both verbal and non-verbal.

If your reflecting back is on-target and sensitively tuned in to your love-mate's heart, he or she will hardly hear you, except perhaps to say "*Yes!*" and then continue sharing even more.

If your reflecting back misses the mark and shows that you are not tuned in, your love-mate's sharing will immediately stop and you will sense awkwardness. You will see your love-mate's obvious distraction as he or she now attempts to digest or respond to *your* comment.

Don't be discouraged by failures. Most people fail most of the time in listening because they are unaware of these listening skills. Practice these skills, however, and you will become an expert listener. You will be amazed at how much you have been missing.

Counselors and therapists are trained to continuously listen and reflect back what they are hearing. It's no wonder that their clients share from the heart so easily, and that so much is revealed for healing.

When you do succeed in listening well, you will see, with great clarity, the empowering effect of your listening on your love-mate. It will feel empowering to you too.

Listen
to your
love-mate's heart
and
watch your love expand

Chapter 7

Perpetual intimacy

Intimacy
unites
us

One afternoon, Shannon gave me one of her playful, daring looks, prompting me to chase her down the hallway of our home.

She ran full speed towards our bedroom.

For some reason known only to Shannon, if she can reach and touch our bed before I catch her, she yells, *"Safe!"* and she has won.

Well, one day she looked at me with that same taunting smile, but I got the jump on her. She was forced to head for the kitchen instead of the bedroom.

"Wait!" she screamed, cornered in the kitchen.

I stopped, thinking something terrible had happened. Shannon raced to grab a pad and pen and furiously began...

"What was she doing?" I wondered. Has some brilliant new idea struck so hard that she doesn't want to lose it?" Before I could even finish my thought, she screamed with delight:

"Safe!"

She had drawn a tiny picture of our bed – the safe zone – and, with a very victorious smile, was touching the bed (in her drawing) with her finger. I had been snookered.

We both had lots of chuckles from that successful little deceit. Needless to say, that ploy worked only once!

Intimacy between love-mates occurs at many levels but always flows from a sense of oneness

In perfect love, this sense of oneness is perpetual because both love-mates bring so much caring and joy to their love lives.

There are, however, great challenges to perpetual intimacy:

♦ Our fast-paced, instant-communication, high-demand, stressful world places enormous pressures on relationships. Where do we find time for intimacy?

♦ Also, after the romance of meeting a love-mate, loving each other, relishing each other's company, and then settling into an enduring relationship and trying to make ends meet financially, how many relationships maintain a high sense of intimacy?

Yet intimacy is what love is all about. That's why we enter love relationships in the first place.

How can love-mates hope to have perpetual intimacy?

Here are some ways:

Take
regular time off
together

Shannon and I both have occupations that call on us every day of the week. How can we possibly have a sense of perpetual intimacy?

From the beginning of our marriage, we decided to take Fridays off as our day alone together. My answering machine says, "Hello, this is Scott and it's Friday, my day to be with my lovely wife Shannon...." She does the same.

It's amazing how people respond to this. My clients not only respect and honor my Fridays with Shannon, but say: "I should do that too!"

It's not easy to shut down "life" and walk-away like this. Think of how tough it is to break loose for a one-week or two-week vacation. In a very real sense, Shannon and I take a vacation every single Friday.

We never quite know what we're going to do on Friday, but we know we will be doing it together – and alone. We never use the day to run errands. It's play day, dream day, think day, share day, pray day, listen day, love day, creative day, quiet day, and movie day all in one.

We often fall into the same pattern, one that brings us great joy – a walk on the beach along the ocean, quiet time to read or talk at one of a few favorite nature spots, our favorite veggie-burgers for lunch at Kirby's overlooking the ocean, and the latest movie (new releases come out Fridays).

But this is not what truly takes place. What really happens on Fridays is that our hearts connect.

It is astounding how much has changed in our lives and thinking in one short week. It is surprising how out-of-tune we are with each other's inner worlds until our hearts have time to unfold in the uninterrupted freedom of our Fridays together.

We connect at the level of each other's desires, fears, doubts, expectations, accomplishments, and forward determinations. It is a day of tremendous sorting out and sharing.

For example, we usually wind up at the beach for one or two hours with a book or article we've been wanting to study. There are long periods of quiet and free thinking. And lots of bouncing ideas off each other, envisioning, discussing, new revelations, laughter, and inner growth. We also find great support on Fridays for the greatest needs confronting each of us.

The forces that would interrupt our taking off Fridays together are enormous, but the pattern we have established has created a pathway to intimacy that is too important to miss. It is no wonder that Shannon and I feel a sense of perpetual intimacy.

This is the intimacy *you* deserve as well!

It doesn't matter whether you are able to take Fridays off together. What matters is that you take time somewhere to be alone and intimate.

Parents, especially, need to make time each week to connect as a couple. Some friends of ours, parents with three young boys, have a standing baby-sitter every Friday night so they can be together alone. Actions like this set a great example for kids of what a loving marriage includes – and also helps fulfill the wonderful reasons that led the couple to make a life together in the first place.

Ask
again (and again),
"What are you thinking, honey?"

This question is so powerful and helpful that it can be sprinkled throughout any day or time together. It brings great clarification and healing to love-mates – and instant intimacy.

Shannon and I ask each other this question all the time. This is not an annoying, prying question when two people love each other. Its real meaning might just as well be phrased:

> *"Sweetie, I'm sitting here loving you and wondering what's cooking in your inner life. If you feel like telling me, I'd love to know. If this isn't a good time, I just want you to know 'I love you.'"*

Imagine how good that question feels when you know that this meaning is behind the words.

A big challenge, however, is that the question often catches us emotionally off-guard and may not be easy to answer. We may be deep in private thought – and happy to be there alone – when we hear this question.

But here's what happens in perfect love. Both love-mates understand the power behind this question to create intimacy. And both love-mates know that the motive behind the question is to stay connected to each other. They knew that this is a moment when they are being called – offered an opportunity – to come to the table of intimacy.

And it's not always easy.

Men, for example, may have greater difficulty than women appreciating this question as an opportunity to be intimate.

- ♦ It may be that men don't want to reveal what is in their private thoughts – for fear their love-mate will disapprove.
- ♦ It may be that men are ashamed of what they are thinking.
- ♦ It may be that men feel too vulnerable sharing feelings without time to think through what they are thinking.
- ♦ It may simply be that men are unaccustomed to sharing in such a way.

Women are much more willing to share feelings and thoughts spontaneously and this freedom of expression strengthens intimacy. Men have a great deal to learn from women on this front.

Understanding this, love-mates help each other warm up to the value and benefits of this question and help each other experience success.

They ask the question in a way that conveys great love, joy, and freedom. They do not let their feelings get hurt by a love-mate's non-answer, slow answer, or shallow answer.

Let this question enter your love life gently. Create as many opportunities for your love-mate to respond in an environment of overwhelming comfort and acceptance.

Hold and touch
each other

Intimacy begs for affection and contact.

In the early stages of love, there is great touching, holding of hands, hugging, embracing, kissing, and love-making.

What happens once love is established? In many cases, love-mates grow distant, separate, apart. There is less holding and touching.

In perfect love, love-mates find perpetual ways to hold and touch each other.

Think how easily you shake hands during the day as you meet person after person. Think how easily you hug a good friend. This is how easily love-mates touch and hold and hug and kiss and embrace each other.

Touching, holding, and embracing
each other
affirms your love

Touching is contagious.

When Shannon's parents came to visit us, we went walking together many places.

"Look at those love-birds," was their first retort as Shannon and I walked along, often hand-in-hand or arm-in-arm. They poked at our intimacy with humor, but it couldn't be stopped. Our intimacy was just too perpetual. The next day we caught them holding hands too!

In fact, Ed and Sis know a whole lot about intimacy. Married together for over 57 years, and both from small towns in Arkansas, they have been known to stop their car by a familiar country bridge and dance to the music of their car radio.

There are so many levels of intimacy.

Love-making is certainly one of them – and a delicate one. Delicate because both love-mates need to feel the same desire for love-making to be fulfilling. Love-making needs to honor *each* love-mate, to tune in to the rhythms of each other's needs.

Intimacy calls forth our greatest sensitivities with a love-mate. Just look at the chapters in this book that have preceded this discussion of intimacy:

♦   A bond of unity
♦   Kindness + Honesty
♦   Cherishing each other's dreams
♦   Genuine equality
♦   Listening to the heart

These are the building blocks that enable intimacy to flourish. Without this foundation, there will be little touching and holding that satisfies the soul.

Perpetual intimacy
is the natural outcome of
the love you deserve

Share
your real life

Genuine intimacy includes the sharing of what is really going on in your life

Intimacy is more than occasional romance.

Think of your life right now. Think of the vast flow of projects, activities, goals, tasks that need to be done, and people to talk to, and....

What percent of all this have you shared with your love-mate? Does your love-mate have any idea what is *really* going on in your life?

It is not easy to unload so much information – even when you want to. It takes time. It takes courage. It takes the right environment. It takes getting past wanting to forget some of it yourself. It takes trusting that your love-mate will understand. It takes believing that your love-mate wants to know.

Despite all these legitimate concerns, sharing your life openly with your love-mate has extraordinary benefits:

♦ Your love-mate will love you even more for your taking the effort to share your world.

♦ In the very process of trying to awkwardly explain to your love-mate your toughest challenge, you will discover solutions you never envisioned.

♦ You will discover great wisdom and originality in your love-mate's responses – for the very reason that he or she is outside the paradigm of your problem.

♦ You will find great comfort and satisfaction in sharing what is in your heart, whether happy, challenging, or terrifying.

♦ You and your love-mate will grow more intimate.

Most men are not too good at sharing their real lives openly. A male colleague I worked with, for example, told me one day that his wife wanted better communication from him when he came home from work.

"I need more words," she told him.

Men, get those words out! Practice revealing your day and thoughts as if a reporter from another planet had just landed in your backyard and was looking to you for insight into an average day on this planet.

Women, don't give up on your love-mate. Way down deep, men are willing to share their hearts. We just don't have anywhere near the confidence you think we do. Or the practice. Or the commitment to talking. And we don't yet trust in the safety of intimacy. Show us how. Let us feel the benefits. Love us towards this new – for us – reality.

Celebrate

your

love

Somehow, through the internet, I managed to set my Seiko pager-watch to send me a message at 8:00 a.m. on the 20th day of each month:

"Happy Anniversary

Scott + Shannon"

By the time you read this book, Shannon and I will have celebrated our 58th anniversary – counting by months, naturally! Why wait a year to celebrate the most important person that has ever walked into my life? It's another opportunity to taste the sweet appreciation that fuels perpetual intimacy.

It doesn't matter whether Shannon and I give each other cards. What matters is that we give each other multiple opportunities to express our love for each other. For one of Shannon's birthdays, I wrote out, in a notebook, 48 reasons why I loved her (see page 244). I didn't think of this as that great a gift, but it surprised me how much she has treasured it.

When was the last time you told your love-mate *why* you loved her or him? Or what you most appreciate about your love-mate?

Use the exercise on the next page to open your heart to your love-mate, or to a good friend.

The top 10 reasons
I love you

1. _____

2. _____

3. _____

4. _____

5. _____

6. _____

7. _____

8. _____

9. _____

10. _____

When we acknowledge
blessings received from another
our hearts rejoice
in
perpetual intimacy

Chapter 8

Empowering manhood

Manhood is undergoing a massive – yet almost invisible – revolution.

Most men, of course, don't talk. That's why this revolution is so invisible.

Almost alone, without much support, men are grappling with what it means to be "a man" as we move towards a millennium that is almost screaming for manhood's consciousness to open up.

Two radically different roads are being presented to men in the privacy of their own consciousness.

The old road – "Power-man" – calls men down the centuries-old path of manhood as the power master of the universe. Men the providers. Men the decision-makers. Men the protectors. Men the leaders.

The new road – "Empowering-man" – calls men forth into a world that is yet to be created. Men the honorers. Men the nurturers. Men the supporters. Men the empowerers of others.

These two roads are not compatible. They do not support each other. As men attempt to straddle both roads simultaneously, without making a clean choice, they can almost feel the foundation of each road disappearing.

Manhood's footing is loose.

On the planet as a whole, unfortunately, only a fraction of men are even aware of these choices. To the misery of themselves and those around them, many men are living out their internal and external lives completely trapped in the "power-man" paradigm. They are so wrapped up in controlling, dominating, and making decisions for others that they are blind to the consequences. Blind, really, to their own way of living.

The consequences for these men in intimate love-relationships are devastating.

An increasing number of men, however, are awakening to the second path – or at least sense the new direction. These men are attempting to carve out a new definition of "real manhood" – but they are doing so without a clear model in mind and without a strong, visible support system that applauds their progress.

Men desperately need a vision of who they are and the great worth they have to contribute to a world progressing at almost breath-taking speed technologically – and turtle-speed in intimate relationships.

> **We are on the**
> **edge**
> **of an historical shift**
> **in the meaning**
> **of**
> **manhood**

We need a vision of manhood that can equal the significance of our civilization's entry into the 21st century. We also need a vision that can open the door for men to an intimate love-life that far exceeds their current experience.

This vision can be summarized in one potent phrase:

Man
_as an_
Empowerer!

To understand this new vision of man as an empowerer, we must first understand why manhood has been trapped – forever, it seems – in the paradigm of power-man.

An intimate look at
"Power-man"

For the vast majority of males on Earth, here's what it's like to grow up "like a man."

Men are socialized to believe in winning

From earliest childhood, boys are expected to win, not lose – whether in baseball, basketball, football, soccer, track, tennis, or a neighborhood game of tag. A man's self-worth goes up with winning, down with losing. Even adult men watching a sports event on TV take sides. They want their side or player to win.

Men are socialized to believe in strength

From their earliest years, boys are expected to be strong. A young man works to develop strength to win in sports. A young man measures his self-worth by the extent of his physical strength.

A man is handed the jar when the top won't give way. A man is expected to move heavy furniture without complaint. Manhood is strength. To lack strength is to lack manhood.

Men are socialized to believe that they are protectors

Young men are expected to protect their sisters or younger brothers. A young man is also expected to protect himself from bullies or enemies, whether he has the skills or not.

A grown-up man is expected to protect his family. A man is also expected to protect his nation from any and all enemies. Men learn that to protect requires the power to dominate – or at least appear to dominate.

Men are socialized to believe that they are providers

Young men know, from an early age, that they will be responsible for providing what is needed to sustain a family.

College, vocational training, and work experiences are known in the heart to be preparation for the real job of being a provider. Every work and learning experience, however part-time or seemingly trivial, is part of the trial of manhood, proving or disproving his capacity to provide.

It doesn't matter that a woman today provides a share, or even a majority, of what is needed. It is still embedded in consciousness, as part of power man's identity, that it is a man's responsibility to provide.

Men are socialized to believe that money is power

Men learn at an early age that it takes money to provide, to protect, to win.

Money is the resource that opens doors. Men see that those with money have power. Men must make money because power is needed to fulfill the obligations of being a man. Making money says to a man that he is worthy.

Men are socialized to believe that they can control any situation

From developing a play on the football field to developing a battle plan that will defeat the enemy, men think in terms of control.

It is their role in life, believe power-men, to control, since control is needed to protect and provide. Man measures his self-worth by the extent that he is in control of his environment and those around him.

Men are socialized to believe that women are inferior

It can't be too much of a surprise, by this point, to understand why power-men would perceive women as inferior. Power-man thinks:

- ♦ Women aren't as strong.
- ♦ They don't provide.
- ♦ They don't protect.
- ♦ They can't control.
- ♦ They don't know how to win.
- ♦ They often don't even want to win.
- ♦ They don't understand the importance of power.

What happens when this "power-man" comes face-to-face with intimate love?

The impotence and danger
of power-man
in intimate love

Intimate love thrives on tenderness, sharing, giving, feeling – not controlling, dominating, speed, and power.

Power-man isn't trained for this. In fact, power-man goes ballistic even thinking of giving up control or power to anyone, even his love-mate. Wouldn't that be weakness? Wouldn't that make him vulnerable? What would be his worth?

It isn't that power-man doesn't want love. It's that love has a different meaning to him. A true love-mate, he reasons, would look up to him, revere his strength, and allow him to remain in control to fulfill his destiny of manhood.

When it comes to sexual interaction, power-man is clear-cut. The object of sex to the power-man is not caressing, closeness, and a sharing of intimacy, but culmination.

Climax is touchdown!

Did he win? Did he provide?

This attitude does not lead to a deepening of intimate love, to mutual satisfaction, or to increasing sensitivity to each other's needs.

It is easy to laugh at "power-man's" attempts to forge an intimate love-relationship. A few TV shows have shown, with great humor, "power-man" stumbling toward a recognition of what real love entails.

Men are, indeed, stumbling towards a new definition of manhood that can survive the challenges of forging a successful intimate love.

But for those power-men who have no plans to change, there is both frustration and danger. This power-man – convinced of his ability to control and the necessity of exercising power over his environment – is a threat to women.

He considers it his choice to do with women what he wishes. He has power. He is trained to control, to dominate, to win.

Even as we look out with a broad Earth-scale view of world consciousness, we see that the raping of women, for example, has been accepted as simply a part of life – in war and peace. Only recently has rape been classified as a crime in war.

The immense tragedy of the power-man mentality so rampant in civilization today begs for transformation. Our intimate love-lives are being tragically short-changed. Our entire world desperately needs a solution – for both men and women.

We need a vision of manhood that can uplift, not destroy, a vision of manhood as empowering, not dominating.

The emerging sense of new manhood

Thousands of men are already making the journey from power-man to a new sense of manhood:

♦ These men have learned to loosen up, to share their feelings, to talk more openly with other men, to value the increasingly significant contribution their wives are making as co-providers (or even lead-providers).

♦ These men are more respectful of women.

♦ These men have outgrown, or are outgrowing, the sense of separation between a man's world and a woman's world.

♦ These men value their own femininity, though they might refer to it as a greater appreciation for tenderness and nurturing combined with their strength.

♦ These men are more deeply involved in raising their kids with qualities of mothering as well as fathering.

♦ These men are having more satisfying intimate love experiences. They are sharing feelings more openly with their love-mates. They are discovering the benefits of intimate love that is mutually satisfying and uplifting.

Even these men, however, are still wrestling with the two worlds – the old power-man who looks increasingly out-of-touch with today's reality, and the new, softer man seeking to harmonize with a world of active, intelligent, contributing women – seeking, in fact, to harmonize with himself and his growing appreciation of a more emotionally-open existence.

This transition is not easy, even for these more liberated men. A steady flow of daily circumstances – at work, in society, in sports, and in private conversations with other men – seek to block the transition to new manhood.

Some men banter politely with the old, power-men they encounter. Some men are more and more repulsed. Others have begun to speak up.

This is the seeding of the revolution in manhood that is overtaking the 21st century. It may be a small beginning, but the shift will have gigantic consequences.

We are witnessing
the emergence
of man
as an
empowerer

What it means

to

empower

To empower means to create an environment for another person to feel, experience, and acquire the full benefits of the power you already possess.

When a coach shows a young man (or woman) the secret of how to correctly execute a play, that is an empowering act. It is empowering because the student, with practice, now has the opportunity to execute that play just as well as the coach.

When a master carpenter teaches a student the secrets of the trade, that is an empowering act. It enables that student to duplicate, and with practice, even excel, the master.

When someone teaches you how to send e-mail, how to create a web-page on the internet, or how to use a computer program, that is an empowering act – because now you can do it too.

Teams are also empowering. Any truly successful basketball team, hostage-rescue team, or business team understands the necessity of combining individual talents and teaching each other the skills necessary for success.

Anyone who has participated in a winning team understands the exhilaration of drawing on each other's strengths to create a flow towards victory.

Successful teams depend on their individual members to empower each other and to teach each other the skills and secrets that will enable them all to perform at a level of grace and excellence.

When it comes to serious power, however, we are less likely to share our knowledge with others. We are fearful that if others learn our secrets, they could displace us, defeat us, or make us vulnerable. This is true in war, in business, and in love. That is why:

To empower another is a courageous act of love and vision

It takes *courage* because an empowerer, rather than seeking to protect or retain power, creates the opportunity for another to gain, possess, and utilize power.

It takes *vision* because an empowerer, rather than fearing loss of power, sees that bringing others into equal power enhances life, business, and love – for the empowerer as well.

It takes *love* because an empowerer looks at the other as deeply worthy of experiencing and enjoying all that the empowerer experiences and enjoys, rather than defining another as a potential enemy that must be blocked from gaining power.

The benefits
of being an empowerer

The benefits of being an empowerer are
enormous:

◆ By teaching another our skills, we refine
with much greater clarity what we know,
or think we know, ourselves. We become
better masters ourselves.

◆ By empowering another, we see the
enormous increase in the other's self-
worth – all from something very easy for
us to do.

◆ By empowering another, we discover
that we can, ourselves, more easily
tackle the problems we have been facing
alone. We become team-builders. The
burden of being the only one responsible
for solutions flows to the team we
ourselves help to forge and empower.
Envision the power and joy of such
teamwork with your love-mate!

◆ By empowering another, we show our
children the meaning of true manhood.

◆ By empowering another, our own self-
worth sky-rockets – because we are far
more richly honored as an empowerer
than as a power-man. We begin to see
the incredible impact of our true power
as empowerers.

◆ By empowering another, we become
more noble!

These are obvious benefits, but much fear and ignorance needs to be overcome to move towards being an empowering man. It takes a consciousness that understands that the benefits of empowering another far exceed the benefits of retaining power.

We live in a civilization that withholds power, hides power, and protects power. To empower another may seem, on the surface, to de-power you. After all, look at all the time and effort and experience it took for you to master and gain power.

Wouldn't you look weaker if another knew your real secrets and could see the vulnerable you? Furthermore, once you empowered another, could you ever gain back exclusive control of that power?

Men who lack true courage and true love resist becoming empowerers. They fear the loss of their privileges and acquisitions more than they appreciate the benefits of providing others with a richer life.

Men who see the vision, however, recognize what an immense opportunity they have to utilize the power they have achieved in ways that will truly uplift their love-mate and the world at large. These men sense the truth:

***To empower others
is the
great opportunity for men
in the
21st century***

The potency of empowering-man

in

intimate love

When a man becomes an empowerer in his intimate love-life, the benefits are extraordinary – to both love-mates.

By seeking to empower his love-mate:

♦ He communicates that he wants his love-mate to enjoy all the benefits of life that he enjoys.

♦ He discovers the immense satisfaction of enabling his love-mate to gain skills and power that he has learned or acquired.

♦ His love-mate feels the strength and depth of his love and sharing and is far more likely to empower back with her own skills and experience.

♦ He releases the burden of thinking that he alone is responsible for providing and protecting.

♦ The bond between love-mates is forged at a higher, more mutually-satisfying level of equality.

♦ He discovers the joy of contributing all that he has learned and gained from typical manhood with his love-mate.

♦ He discovers the immensity of the impact of empowering his love-mate and sees the potential for this on a wider, world scale.

Becoming an empowerer
of your love-mate
raises
your love life
to a
new
dimension

Here are six steps that will help you become an expert empowerer:

- ◆ Decide to be an empowerer.
- ◆ Identify those who have most empowered you.
- ◆ Identify ways you can empower your love-mate.
- ◆ Start empowering.
- ◆ Practice empowering in love-making.
- ◆ Identify even more ways to empower your love-mate

Let's look at these in detail.

Decide
to be
an empowerer

It is not difficult to become an empowerer once you make the decision.

The key is to unself your motivation.

If your motivation is primarily to impress your love-mate with your skills, you will fall short. An empowering man seeks to have his love-mate impressed by what *she* can do as a result of his empowering.

If your motivation is simply to have a higher sense of worth yourself, you will also fall short. The higher goal is to enable *your love-mate* to have a higher sense of worth.

If your motivation is to truly enable your love-mate to understand, practice, and master whatever power you have to share, your love-mate will feel the underlying genuineness of your motivation and your empowering will be successful.

An empowering man looks for ways he can empower his love-mate.

Liberation,
not domination,
is the goal of an empowering man
in perfect love

Identify
those who have
most empowered you

Who are the top three people in your whole life who have most empowered you?

1. _____
2. _____
3. _____

What are the most significant things these people did to empower you?

♦ _____
♦ _____
♦ _____
♦ _____
♦ _____

Let these skills be your model as you move towards empowering expertise.

Here are my empowerers-of-my-life awards:

One man, Carl Rogers, has had an enormously empowering impact on my life – and I never met him. He wrote books that so clearly explained how to empathize that I felt he was instructing me personally. I attribute my listening skills to what he taught me. I am changed. He handed me his talent.

Shannon, my treasure of a love-mate, is the most empowering woman I have ever met. It is not just that she loves me. Or that we have so much fun together. She has taught me, and shown me, how to think out from such heights of metaphysical truth and powerful affirmations that my entire consciousness has been elevated to a whole new view of well-being. I am changed. She handed me her talent.

My third choice for the empowerer-of-my-life award goes to my Mom. She showed me, by her example, what it means to love another while simultaneously standing for principle. She handed me her talent. Here is one of her favorite lines:

> *Act,*
> *don't react*

Identify

ways you can empower

your love-mate

Now that you are thinking of yourself as an empowerer, ask yourself:

- What power do I most prize in my own life?
- Does my love-mate have this power?
- What other information or skills do I have that would most benefit my love-mate?
- What power – information, knowledge, or skills – does my love-mate most desire?

If you don't know, ask your love-mate. You might be surprised by her answers. Even if you think you know, ask. You'll still be surprised!

***An empowerer
is constantly looking for ways
to empower his
love-mate***

Start

empowering

Start practicing, with your love-mate, the skills you have learned from the top three empowerers-of-your-life.

For example, when Shannon and I first married, she had little computer experience. I love computers and my professional experience has given me wide expertise with many computer programs. Here, I realized, was a wonderful opportunity to share what I had learned with Shannon. My goal was to help *her* become an expert, not to do work for her.

It wasn't without a struggle. When Shannon would reach a point of *"I can't take any more learning right now,"* we laughed (most of the time) and stopped. But she knew I was there as a resource, that I would not withhold secrets, and that she could draw on my expertise at her convenience. That itself was empowering. Today, she is independently competent with her computer.

Here's another example. I love conducting workshops as well as teaching others how to conduct them. One day, a new workshop instructor was struggling to learn a presentation. She kept losing confidence and falling apart in the middle of her presentation.

I suggested that we go to a private classroom and that she practice her presentation until she succeeded. We did, but after three additional failures, she left the room in tears.

I waited.

In a few minutes, she came back, and did it again – successfully! My belief in her ability, my patience in letting her worth come to the surface, and my providing a safe environment in which to practice and fail was the empowering she needed.

Here's another excellent way to tune in to your love-mate's needs and be an empowerer. Ask your love-mate, *"On a scale of 1 to 10, to what extent do you feel empowered by me?"* The mere asking of this question – if genuine – is empowering to a love-mate.

If your love-mate says "8", don't breathe easily and go back to your own world. Ask the key follow-up question, *"What would make it a 10?"* Now you'll get some real answers. You may not like them, but remember, your goal isn't to feel self-satisfied but for your love-mate to feel empowered. This exercise is about your love-mate's well-being, not yours.

Be prepared to be surprised by what your love-mate truly desires. You may be providing a car, income for maintaining the family, and a whole lot more, but your love-mate may want something as simple as being treated as an equal decision-maker.

Another way to learn about empowering is to put yourself in the role of the one being empowered. Ask your love-mate to teach you something that you truly want to learn. What power, knowledge, or skills do you most wish you could have from your love-mate? Ask your love-mate to empower you in this area.

Just this asking (if honest) will empower your love-mate – because it says that you find your love-mate highly valuable to you.

By letting your love-mate empower you, you will also learn how it feels to be the one empowered. It often feels awkward, frustrating, and debilitating to be the one being empowered because the spotlight is on our weakness. Learn from this how to be a better, clearer, more patient empowerer yourself.

Practice empowering
in love-making

Love-making calls forth the highest skills of empowering – listening, tuning in, connecting, and being at one with each other.

What does your love-mate truly want in love-making – gratification, caressing, or perhaps just close emotional time together?

True love-making is not some momentary act disconnected from the rest of your relationship.

Love-making
that empowers
occurs when two love-mates
are so united in spirit
that they
sense and satisfy
each other's intimate needs

Are your love-actions based on meeting your needs, or empowering your love-mate?

To truly empower your love-mate, you need to tune in to his or her desires, needs, feelings, fears, concerns, and hopes. Discuss these openly – and be ready to learn a lot about your love-mate's inner heart. Otherwise, you will give your love-mate what *you* think is appropriate. This, in all honesty, is domination and the exercise of power rather than the gift of enabling and empowering.

Put those listening skills in gear!

Identify

even more ways

to empower your love-mate

Now that you are practicing being an empowerer, dig even deeper. Are there even more ways to empower your love-mate?

For example, after Shannon and I married, I realized her intense desire to write articles in her area of life-passion – healing. She had brilliant, original ideas pouring out of her consciousness, but wasn't confident in writing and editing.

Since I brought to our love-relationship many years of professional editing and writing experience, here was a perfect opportunity for me to practice empowering.

We both remember her first article. By the third round of editing, she was about to forget the whole thing. She didn't realize how important editing was to great writing. It's never easy to learn new skills, but when someone teaches us the "secrets" of success in any area of life, it can change the course of our entire life.

Shannon has not only published numerous articles, but now loves to write – and edit. And there is a powerful moral to this story. Today, Shannon is my top editor – and she is one excellent editor! This is a perfect example of the true benefit of empowering. What started out as a blessing to Shannon became an even bigger blessing to me.

***Empowering another
always returns
the most benefits to the
empowerer***

Self-quiz
Empowering manhood

Directions: Rate yourself on how well you express empowering manhood. If you are a woman, rate your love-mate, or rate the degree to which you, yourself, express empowering manhood.

1. I value empowering manhood:

    1   2   3   4   5   6   7   8   9   10

    Not at all   To some degree   Completely

2. I empower my love-mate by sharing my most valuable skills:

    1   2   3   4   5   6   7   8   9   10

    Not at all   To some degree   Completely

3. I empower my love-mate in love-making:

    1   2   3   4   5   6   7   8   9   10

    Not at all   To some degree   Completely

4. I empower my love-mate's dreams:

    1   2   3   4   5   6   7   8   9   10

    Not at all   To some degree   Completely

5. I constantly look for new ways to empower my love-mate:

    1   2   3   4   5   6   7   8   9   10

    Not at all   To some degree   Completely

Self-rating

Empowering manhood

Total Score: _____ divided by 5 = _____

1-2   Empowering vacuum. Time for radical revision or new possibilities.

3-4   Minimal empowering.   Time for you to set higher standards.

5-6   Survivable empowering. Is this acceptable to you for the rest of your life?

7-8   Decent empowering. Why not go for the gold? Ask yourself: What would make this a 10?

9-10   Genuine empowering. Rejoice!

Chapter 9

Self-empowered womanhood

Womanhood, like manhood, is on the edge of a millennium advance.

While men are grappling with the transition from "power-man" to "empowering-man," women are simultaneously moving towards a redefinition of their highest identity as we catapult into a new century of opportunity.

Women are
already experts
at empowering others

The very core of womanhood is her nurturing expertise – her ability to enable *others* to succeed. Just think of any women who come to mind. Empowering others is as natural to most women as exercising power is to most men. The immense opportunity now facing womanhood is to turn her nurturing expertise inward and empower *herself.*

The challenge for womanhood
in the 21st century
can be summarized in one word
–
Self-empowerment!

There is enormous resistance to the full empowerment of womanhood:

- ♦ Civilization for centuries has placed womanhood in second place.
- ♦ Because of her own immense dedication to empowering *others,* a woman's dreams, needs, and ambitions are often put on hold, relegated to second place, or ignored – by herself.
- ♦ Most men are not yet advanced enough in their millennium consciousness to encourage (or demand) self-empowered womanhood.
- ♦ Women are torn between conflicting roles of mothering, what kind of "man" they want, and their professional development.

This combined consciousness adds up to an enormous wall of repression to empowered womanhood – but this wall is crumbling.

Empowered womanhood is so vital to a woman's expanding consciousness of identity, to her ability to experience perfect love, and to the success of millennium civilization that women must take leadership of their own empowerment.

Women themselves must be the leaders of their own empowerment

To understand the enormous challenge in consciousness facing womanhood, it is vital to confront the true status of womanhood today on our planet. Empowered womanhood has come too far towards the light to live any longer in fog.

Womanhood
stubbornly subordinate

Yes, there has been progress:

- Many – but not all – women can now vote.
- Women now contribute substantially to family income.
- Women hold more positions of political power than ever before in history.
- There are laws against discrimination of women – in some countries.
- Women leaders and writers have eloquently proclaimed women's dignity and worth.

Despite these gains, womanhood remains stubbornly subordinate:

- Most women still earn less than men – for the same work.
- Abuse and violence against women is still widespread.
- Sexual discrimination against women still exists.
- Women represent only 11% of seats in legislatures around the world.
- The Equal Rights Amendment, which affirmed a woman's right to equality in the United States, could not gather the required support to become law.
- Women in many parts of our planet have almost no rights – or only those rights granted by men.

Why should women, who comprise 51% of the Earth's population, live at a lower level of honoring, dignity, worth, opportunity, and power than men?

This is a travesty of history. Mankind's expanding, spiritual consciousness can no longer tolerate this condition – not for another century or another decade!

Looking objectively at the condition of women today on Earth, an observer visiting from another planet would report back that our civilization is undergoing a slow transition from "Subordinate womanhood" – women regarded as subordinate, subservient, and second-class – to "Empowered womanhood" – women experiencing genuine equality and in charge of their own destiny.

Unfortunately, for most women and men, the enormous shift in consciousness needed to end this reign of subordination is barely present or apparent in our daily thoughts and lives.

Why this absence of absolute rebellion?

Because the weight of thousands of years of repression of women is such a norm of consciousness that it is like breathing air. We breath air because we were born breathing it. It is what we do. We don't question it.

Women have been raised, for centuries, breathing repression. And men, for centuries, have been raised thinking of women as secondary. Few question whether this is appropriate or just. It is simply the nature of their lives.

The transition from subordinate woman to self-empowered woman is slow because there is still no bold, widely-adopted vision of a higher goal for womanhood as we enter the millennium.

This is true despite countless women's organizations that have passionately, eloquently, and factually articulated the problems facing women.

For women – and enlightened men – this status of womanhood on our planet today is unacceptable! Our advancing consciousness knows that this is wrong.

Yet how many women or men do you know who have a clear sense of the empowered role women are destined to fulfill in the 21st century?

Do you?

The inevitability of empowered womanhood

Millennium consciousness is forcing open the doors of our civilization's thought.

We all sense this. We sense a shift – something momentous – emerging in universal consciousness. We've seen this before:

- Nothing could stop the freeing of slaves.
- Nothing could stop the movement to grant women the right to vote.
- Nothing could stop the Civil Rights Movement.

These movements succeeded because they represented universal truth and spiritual justice.

This is exactly why nothing can stop the movement to empowered womanhood.

> *Empowered womanhood*
> *represents*
> *universal truth*
> *and*
> *spiritual justice*

We know this in our hearts. We may not know *how* it is to be achieved, but an increasing minority (growing towards a majority – and including men) feel the power of this idea. The light of this truth is penetrating the entrenched barricades of centuries of repression.

> *The rise to*
> *empowered womanhood*
> *is inevitable*

Let us establish a vision so clear, so illuminating, so passionate, and so full of spiritual truth and justice that the vision creates a landslide of consciousness that crumbles the walls of ignorance, repression, and unwillingness to give up established practices of abuse, domination, and control.

Let each of us
envision womanhood
in her empowered stature and glory
as we enter the 21st century

Looking
from the future
to envision

Hold on to your mind.

Or rather, let loose your mind!

Let's envision together the transitions that will *inevitably* take place with womanhood before the year 2098 – 100 years from the first publication of this book.

I'll start and you can add to the list:

♦ The United States will have elected at least 5 women Presidents during the 25 elections from the years 2000 - 2100.

♦ The United States will have elected at least 10 women Vice-Presidents during the same century.

♦ Women in legislative positions on our planet will have risen from 11% to 50%.

♦ 50% of leadership positions on Earth – including the United Nations – will be held by women.

♦ Divorces will have dropped from over 50% to under 20% as men and women shape their lives in a mental environment of empowered opportunity, mutual trust, and more open communication.

♦ Children will grow up in a mental environment that equally honors empowered womanhood and empowering manhood.

♦ The concept of *power* in civilization will
    have been largely redefined – with the
    help of self-empowered women and
    empowering men – from win-lose control
    to win-win partnership.

What would you add to the list?

♦ _____

♦ _____

♦ _____

♦ _____

♦ _____

♦ _____

♦ _____

Were you forced outside the confines of your
present-day consciousness of womanhood as you
moved through this exercise?

Were you able to glimpse the *mental* lock of
limitation on your present consciousness?

Albert Einstein's brilliant words help us grasp
the importance of breaking loose from our limited
thinking about womanhood as we enter a millennium shift taking place in our consciousness:

"Problems cannot be solved
at the same level of awareness
that created them"

A new level of awareness
of womanhood

Here is a potent question that breaks through the crust of accumulated thinking about womanhood and magnifies her immense value:

What would our civilization
be like
if women
did not exist?

◆ Where would our children turn for mothering?

◆ Who would teach our children?

◆ Would there be any children?

◆ Where would we find warmth, praise, encouragement, and nurturing for our dreams?

◆ How would we fill the vacuum of the loss of a woman's love?

◆ Where would we find the lost insight that women bring to the issues that confront our lives and civilization?

◆ Where would we be without the women who comprise 51% of the population on our planet?

◆ Where would we be without the 136 women (listed on the next page) who have been named to the National Women's Hall of Fame in the United States?

The National Women's Hall of Fame

Bella Abzug
Abigail Adams
Jane Addams
Louisa May Alcott
Ethel Percy Andrus
Marian Anderson
Susan B. Anthony
Virginia Apgar
Ella Baker
Ann Bancroft
Clara Barton
Mary McLeod Bethune
Antionette Blackwell
Elizabeth Blackwell
Amelia Bloomer
Margaret Bourke-White
Myra Bradwell
Mary Breckinridge
Gwendolyn Brooks
Pearl S. Buck
Charlotte Anne Bunch
St. Frances Zavier Cabrini
Annie Jump Cannon
Rachel Carson
Mary Cassatt
Willa Cather
Carrie Chapman Catt
Shirley Chisholm
Jacqueline Cochran
Eileen Collins
Ruth Colvin
Jane Cunningham Croly
Emily Dickenson

Dorothea Dix
Elizabeth Hanford Dole
Anne Dallas Dudley
Amelia Earhart
Catherine East
Mary Baker Eddy
Marian Wright Edelman
Gertrude Belle Elion
Alie Evans
Geraldine Ferraro
Ella Fitzgerald
Betty Friedan
Margaret Fuller
Matilda Joslyn Gage
Lillian Moller Gilbreth
Charlotte Perkins Gilman
Dr. Maria Goeppert Mayer
Ella Grasso
Martha Griffiths
Mary A. Hallaren
Fannie Lou Hamer
Alice Hamilton
Helen Hayes
Mary Harris "Mother Jones"
Dorothy Height
Oveta Culp Hobby
Wilhelmina Cole Holladay
Grace Hopper
Dolores Huerta
Helen Hunt
Zora Neale Hurston
Anne Hutchinson
Mary Jacobi
Frances Wisebart Jacobs

Mae Jemison
Barbara Jordan
Helen Keller
Nanneri O. Keohane
Billie Jean King
Maggie Kuhn
Suzette La Flesche
Anne Morrow Lindbergh
Belva Lockwood
Juliette Gordon Low
Mary Lyon
Mary Mahoney
Wilma Mankiller
Barbara McClintock
Louise McManus
Margaret Mead
Maria Mitchell
Constance Baker Motley
Lucretia Mott
Antonio Novello
Annie Oakley
Sandra Day O'Connor
Georgia O'Keeffe
Rosa Parks
Alice Paul
Frances Perkins
Esther Peterson
Jeannette Rankin
Ellen Swallow Richards
Linda Richards
Sally Ride
Eleanor Roosevelt
Ernestine Louise Potowski Rose
Sister Elaine Roulet
Wilma Rudolph
Josephine St. Pierre Ruffin

Florence Sabin
Margaret Sanger
Katherine Siva Saubel
Betty Bone Schiess
Patricia Schroeder
Mother Elizabeth Seton
Florence Seibert
Muriel Siebert
Bessie Smith
Margaret Chase Smith
Hannah Greenebaum Solomon
Elizabeth Cady Stanton
Gloria Steinem
Nettie Stevens
Lucy Stone
Harriet Beecher Stowe
Maria Tallchief
Helen Brook Taussig
Sojourner Truth
Harriet Tubman
William D. Wald
Madam C.J. Walker (Sarah Breedlove)
Faye Wattleton
Ida B. Wells-Barnett
Oprah Winfrey
Sarah Winnemucca
Fanny Wright
Rosalyn Yalow
Gloria Yerkovich
Edith Wharton
Mildred "Babe" Ditrickson Zaharias

♦ Or the 21 women inducted into the National Women's Hall of Fame in 1998: Madeleine Albright, Maya Angelou, Lydia Bradley, Dr. Mary Calderone, Mary Shadd Cary, Elizabeth Cochrane (Nellie Bly), Joan Cooney, Gerty Radnitz Cori, Sarah Grimke, Angelina Grimke Weld, Julia Howe, Dr. Shirley Jackson, Dr. Shannon Lucid, Katharine McCormick, Ambassador Rozanne Ridgway, Edith Rogers. Felice Schwartz, Eunice Kennedy Shriver, Beverly Sills, Florence Wald, Chien-Shiung Wu.

♦ How many more women of great value can you name?

Is your appreciation of womanhood expanding?

The issue is not
whether womanhood
is
more valuable than manhood

—

The issue is
whether womanhood
is
equally *valuable*

Let us envision what will happen when civilization lets loose the chains of mental subordination and supports empowered womanhood.

Empowered womanhood
will be cherished for her glory
and infinite worth

We see more and more references today to God as feminine – in our literature, sermons, conversations with others, and in our own consciousness.

This is the natural outcome of defining God as Love. Divine Love brings us directly to Womanhood, for womanhood expresses the purity, essence, and brilliance of Love. This is the true foundation of Womanhood, the basis from which her radiance pours forth.

As women
see themselves as the
spiritual expression of Love,
they will feel the
power
of their
healing identity

As men, too, come to see women as the embodiment of this highest Power, they will grow in their admiration and support of empowered womanhood.

In truth, empowered womanhood and empowering manhood are not restricted by gender, but embrace all men and all women:

Empowered womanhood
and empowering manhood
are within each of us!

Empowered womanhood
will exercise her power
to shape
millennium civilization

All civilization feels the immense power of a woman's nurturing expertise, whether from a mother, love-mate, or friend.

A mother's love, for example, is generally unconditional. It sticks by us even when we stray. It never casts us off. It remains and loves us. It calms, soothes, praises, encourages, and blesses. It remembers our innate goodness.

This nurturing is a great force – a massive power in our lives – and it is now being called forth to uplift our entire civilization.

The time has come
for women to become
power-nurturers

–

not just
for their offspring or love-mates,
but for themselves
and the
world

That same observer from another planet who sees Earth as moving through a transition from subordinate woman to empowered woman also sees enormous destruction taking place on Earth as fighting between religious groups, ethnic groups, and opposing cultures rampages world peace.

The Earth's people are emotionally starving – silently and audibly crying to be lifted out of repression, fear, starvation, domination, and abuse and lifted into a nurturing, caring, honoring, empowering environment.

Our world needs women as consciousness-leaders!

Women intuitively know what our world so desperately needs. Women *have* the consciousness and skills of empowering others that can bring harmony to centuries of entrenched hatred, fear, abuse, and rebellion.

Our entire civilization is in great need of the unleashed strength of womanhood.

The entire Earth is today womanhood's most important child

As women come to see themselves in the brilliant light of empowered identity and *exercise* their full womanhood, everyone will benefit:

- ♦ Women will feel the joy and satisfaction of seeing their true identity honored and utilized – without restriction.
- ♦ Men will see world-wide problems dissolving under the healing influence of womanhood's love, intuition, and empowering strength.
- ♦ Our planetary home will become a stronger, safer, more compassionate environment for us all.

Empowered womanhood
will
redefine power

Women have spent lifetimes – centuries and centuries – cherishing, honoring, encouraging, uplifting, helping, and empowering their offspring and love-mates.

As women enter the 21st century with a clear vision of empowered womanhood, it is inevitable that women will help civilization redefine power.

This new consciousness will define power as the ability to uplift, nurture, honor, and empower, not to dominate, control, or keep oppressed, and this new understanding will lift all mankind to a higher model of power.

It is of immense significance that the revolution taking place in male consciousness is simultaneously opening to this same redefinition of power.

The emerging unity
of
male and female consciousness
on the value of empowering others
will propel
our planet's entrance to
millennium
consciousness

Empowered womanhood
will provide
spiritual vision

Womanhood's enormous spiritual power is coming forward.

Mary Baker Eddy, the powerful spiritual healer, defined God as "Father-Mother." Mother Teresa showed us the meaning of compassion. Princess Diana revealed the universal heart of spiritual love. Marianne Williamson, Gloria Copeland, Oprah Winfrey, and Maya Angelou – and many other women today – point us towards light.

Our civilization is hungering for womanhood's spiritual guidance. Millennium consciousness is awakening to the great contribution of womanhood to our well-being as a civilization.

The moment has arrived
for womanhood
to rise to the consciousness
of her immense worth
and exercise
her spiritual talents
with self-empowered
authority

The moment has also come for men to cherish womanhood's spiritual power and welcome it into their lives.

Self-empowered women
will experience
the love they deserve

As a woman lives her life from the consciousness of self-empowered womanhood and cherishes her spiritual authority and immense value to civilization, her love life will expand into the glory it deserves!

Imagine the benefits that an empowered woman brings to intimate love:

- ♦ She feels the freedom of being able to make her own choices free of fear, domination, or control by a man.
- ♦ She does not fall for a love-mate who will hold her back from her life mission.
- ♦ She exudes confidence and strength.
- ♦ She loves and admires herself for being true to herself and expressing her identity so fully and so well.
- ♦ Her self-worth is at a *sustained* high.
- ♦ She is an expert at empowering herself and feels the powerful strength this brings to her identity and love life.

Enlightened men are going to fall crazy in love with women so liberated, so self-honoring, and so empowering.

And yes, women, these men exist!

To accept less from a man will erode your true identity.

***Any man
who doesn't honor
self-empowered womanhood
will do nothing
but hold down or hold back
– forever –
an empowered woman***

Empowering men are surfacing, and these men want relationships with empowered women. The benefits to a man of an empowered woman are enormous:

- ♦ He can share life in a genuine part-nership with an equal, strong, confident love-mate. Rather than living with a sense of singular responsibility and burden, he can experience teamwork, satisfaction, and mutual liberation.

- ♦ He knows he has a love-mate with the confidence, self-understanding, and em-powering skills needed to help him tackle any challenge in his life.

- ♦ He will experience love-making at a higher level of satisfaction, freedom, and mutual empowering.

So, the big question is not what empowered womanhood is, or whether it has enormous benefits, but:

***How is the vision of
empowered womanhood
going to happen
in your life?***

Here are some bold steps you can take:

Decide

to be

an empowered woman

This is not as obvious a decision as you might think.

- ♦ Some women may say *"Yes!"* but still want the advantages of being protected and provided for, even if this means being subordinate.

- ♦ Many women are still unaccustomed to power. Being self-empowered moves the balance of power towards equality, and this shift transforms almost every facet of an intimate love-relationship.

Where do *you* stand – internally – in the great awakening of self-empowered womanhood?

If you had been alive a hundred years ago, would you have been an advocate for a woman's right to vote? Or would you have questioned the value of such a bold, empowering step for women?

Would you have suggested we move forward cautiously? Or boldly?

This is the choice today you face in your intimate love-life.

You have the power
to raise
your love life
to a level that honors empowered womanhood

–

Will you do it?
When?

Here's a test situation. Let's say you have identified the top 10 qualities you are looking for in a love partner, and "an empowering man who honors empowered womanhood" is one of the 10 requirements.

Now suppose a very appealing man comes along who scores 7 out of 10 on your love list. Unfortunately, being an empowerer and honoring empowered womanhood is not on his agenda.

Would you say to yourself: *"Go for it, seven out of ten is not that bad. I may never get more."*

Or would you say to yourself:

"Nothing is going to prevent me from experiencing an empowering man who honors empowered womanhood!"

The big question is not, "Are you willing to lose the man?" The defining question is, "Are you willing to give up your empowered womanhood?"

Imagine yourself rising to the level of self-honoring where you could say to this potential love-mate:

> *"There is a whole lot that appeals to me about you, but I'm not willing to settle for a man who does not know how to honor womanhood or have an empowering relationship."*

Suppose your potential love partner slinks away in the face of your boldness, rather than opening himself to a higher sense of empowered womanhood and empowering manhood.

Even if he finds another woman who allows him to have all the power, will he be satisfied? In his private consciousness, he is bound to think:

"I really liked that woman (you) who rejected me. She had a lot more substance."

Now envision the impact if, today, a thousand women in your community said to their potential love-mates:

"There is a whole lot that appeals to me about you, but I'm not willing to settle for a man who does not know how to honor womanhood or have an empowering relationship."

These men may not be too pleased, but they are going to begin examining the benefits of changing, and start asking, *"What is this empowering man and empowered womanhood that these women want?"*

Never underestimate the large-scale consequences of your individual love-actions

Are your love-actions empowering womanhood, or maintaining the status quo of subordination?

Your inner commitment that the love you deserve includes an empowering man sends out a message to the entire universe. And the universe will respond.

If you are committed to an empowering love-relationship, you will experience it

That may seem an outrageously bold statement, but it is a true statement.

This is part of your own empowering – to recognize that the values you treasure in your private heart will exude from your being. All those around you – including men who are empowerers – will feel your strength and be drawn to your higher sense of identity.

Identify
your highest and best use
as an
empowered woman

In real estate, an excellent method of assessing the value of a parcel of ground is to identify its "highest and best use." Would it be most valuable as a park, a home, a parking lot, a church, or an apartment complex?

Using the same thought-process, how would you define *your* highest and best use as a self-empowered, individual woman?

Think about this carefully. What would give you the greatest sense of fulfillment as an empowered woman?

♦ _____

♦ _____

♦ _____

♦ _____

♦ _____

This is the
self-empowered woman
within you
to
protect, support, nurture, empower,
express, and love

Demand
a love partner
who will support your
highest and most valuable identity

We so much want to be loved that we are tempted to settle for less than we deserve.

♦ Do you deserve to experience self-empowered womanhood in your *entire* life? Yes!

♦ Do you deserve to experience self-empowered womanhood in your love-life? Yes!

That's your mental position. It is a position of self-empowerment.

You will never lose real love by taking this full-force mental position. All you will lose is the opportunity to be abused, controlled, manipulated, dominated, or unappreciated. Too much is at stake for you to settle for a love-mate who is not an empowerer.

The love-mate
you deserve
honors
self-empowered womanhood

Put
your life
in first place

This can be a challenging step since it is history's legacy for a woman to support her man, to support her children, and to wait for her turn.

> **Womanhood
> needs to exaggerate
> putting her life in first place
> even to approximate balance
> with a man**

It is not selfish to put your life in first place. This does not mean abandoning your husband or your children. What it does mean is not abandoning *you!*

For example, in writing this book, it was natural for me to think through the zillions of steps that would finally result in your actually holding this book. Like a General organizing troops, equipment, supplies, and resources for a battle, I moved forward with relish. And I not only asked Shannon for support, but I needed it! Her encouragement, wisdom, editing, and belief in me were critical to my success.

One day, however, the whole process crashed inward as Shannon and I both realized that she was being swept away from *her* life priorities. It was the most natural thing for her to love and support me so richly, but my priority had put her lifepath priorities way down in second place.

Not only had I allowed this to happen, but Shannon herself had allowed this to happen.

It wasn't until I was writing this chapter that the full realization of what had happened occurred to me. My motives had not been unloving to Shannon. I was simply enthusiastic about *my* priorities.

The moment this realization hit home, I took back my book from Shannon's desk and asked her to stop editing and dig into her own life priorities, which are every bit as significant and valuable as mine.

Shannon had come to the same conclusion almost simultaneously. Though it caused some disruption, we made the change immediately. We value each other so thoroughly that we leap to make such corrections when needed – and this was a much needed correction.

Even though I support empowered womanhood, here was a perfect example of where I had fallen short. The lesson, for Shannon, was clear:

Women must take responsibility
for keeping their needs
equal
to a man's

Be the engine
of your own
self-empowerment

When you think of attracting a love-mate – or even more fully attracting your present love partner – are you *waiting* to be appreciated, loved, valued, and wanted?

Self-empowered womanhood abandons this unempowering status of waiting for a prince to recognize her beauty.

Self-empowered womanhood
is already beautiful

–

already complete

This is the consciousness of womanhood in perfect love. She knows her worth. She knows her intrinsic beauty. She loves her life. She loves herself.

No one can hand this power to her. As womanhood perceives that she *has* this power, it will exude from her life with grace and authority.

Be a role-model

of

self-empowered womanhood

Who are the three women *in history* you most admire?

- ♦ _____
- ♦ _____
- ♦ _____

Who are the three women *you know today* that you most admire?

- ♦ _____
- ♦ _____
- ♦ _____

Why do you admire these women? What do they have in common?

- ♦ _____
- ♦ _____
- ♦ _____
- ♦ _____
- ♦ _____

To what extent are these women leaders, creators, executors of their own dreams, and satisfied, self-empowered women?

You are a role model for all womanhood

Yes, *you* are a role-model. The only question is, what kind of womanhood are you modeling?

Let's say you are a mother with a young son and a young daughter and dedicated to raising the best children possible:

- ♦ Are you raising your son to be an empowering man?
- ♦ Are you raising your daughter to be a self-empowered woman?
- ♦ What are you teaching each of them about womanhood?

These are millennium questions, because the millennium will be shaped by your sons and daughters

Even if you gave this book to your son and daughter and had them read it every single year until they were twenty-five and happily receiving the love they deserve, the impact of this book would pale in comparison with the impact of your life example of womanhood.

For example, think of a mother who perceives herself as simply taking care of the kids and home, while her husband "works." Compare that mother with one who sees herself as the CEO (chief executive officer) of the home front and a millennium role-model for her kids.

The first mother is likely to *feel* that she is in a second place status, and her kids will learn from *her* consciousness this status of womanhood.

The second mother *feels* like a CEO and her sons and daughters will *see* a self-empowered woman in action. A CEO defines the mission, motivates others to see the vision, trains, delegates, and executes.

**The key
is not in what a woman does,
but
how she
perceives herself**

Think, too, of a professional woman. Does she perceive herself to be in second place, waiting for her turn, or does she think of herself as the CEO of her own destiny?

**You are the
CEO
of your own womanhood**

Love yourself
as a self-empowered woman

Let your new sense of identity as a confident, self-empowered woman exude from your consciousness and life activities:

♦ Practice living in the consciousness of empowered womanhood.

♦ Practice loving in the consciousness of a self-empowered woman.

♦ Let your self-empowered womanhood do the attracting of a love-mate.

♦ Practice using your self-empowered skills with your love-mate, your friends, your family – everywhere.

*It is your
inherent right
to experience
self-empowered womanhood
in every aspect
of your life*

Self-quiz
Self-empowered womanhood

Directions: Rate yourself on how well you express self-empowered womanhood. If you are a man, rate your love-mate, or rate the degree to which you, yourself, express self-empowered womanhood.

1. I value self-empowered womanhood:

    1   2   3   4   5   6   7   8   9   10
    Not at all   To some degree   Completely

2. I value and demand a love-mate who honors and supports empowered womanhood:

    1   2   3   4   5   6   7   8   9   10
    Not at all   To some degree   Completely

3. I put myself in first place equally to putting my love-mate in first place:

    1   2   3   4   5   6   7   8   9   10
    Not at all   To some degree   Completely

4. I am the engine of my own self-empowerment:

    1   2   3   4   5   6   7   8   9   10
    Not at all   To some degree   Completely

5. I love myself as a self-empowered woman:

    1   2   3   4   5   6   7   8   9   10
    Not at all   To some degree   Completely

Self-rating
Self-empowered womanhood

Total Score: _____ divided by 5 = _____

1-2   Self-empowered vacuum. Time for radical revision or new possibilities.

3-4   Minimal self-empowering. Time for you to set higher standards.

5-6   Survivable self-empowering. Is this acceptable to you for the rest of your life?

7-8   Decent self-empowering. Why not go for the gold? What would make this a 10?

9-10   Genuine self-empowering. Rejoice!

Chapter 10

Loving yourself Perfectly

How well do you love yourself?

1	2	3	4	5	6	7	8	9	10
Not at all				Somewhat					Completely

Despite years of education and life experience, most of us fail miserably in learning to love ourselves.

This great loss takes place within our private consciousness, hidden from the world – hidden even from the people who think they know us best. We are masters at hiding ourselves.

My average, life-time self-rating on loving myself is probably just under 7. Not great, but not terrible. During my previous marriages, it was closer to 4. That definitely qualifies for lousy. Today, I'm grateful that I can rate myself at 9 and edging up.

*The struggle
to love ourselves
is vital to our well-being
and our love life*

When we allow ourselves to live without loving ourselves, we sentence ourselves to an isolated prison cell of self-love deprivation. Unfortunately, most of us are mean to ourselves. We refuse to grant ourselves pardon – or even parole – from our own imprisonment.

In truth, your rating of how much you love yourself reflects the degree to which you *hate* yourself. The word *hate* may seem too powerful, but it wakens us to reality.

How can we possibly *love* our love-mate well, while we *hate* ourselves – or even while we are neutral in loving ourselves? We cannot.

To give or receive perfect love, we must love ourselves boldly

All the energy you are using in hate or dislike of yourself is lost energy for loving your love-mate. How can we even calculate the immensity of this loss of love – for ourselves, our love-mates, and for civilization!

It is time to learn how to give ourselves the love we deserve

–

from ourselves

Let's uncover the enormous impact of what would happen in your life – and love-life – if you loved yourself well.

Take some self-honoring time and fill in the *Top 10 Ways to Love Myself Perfectly* quiz on the next page.

Promise that you will not continue reading this book until you have identified at least *ten* things you would be doing or thinking if you loved yourself perfectly right now. To ensure compliance, this book is designed to self-destruct if you attempt to read ahead without completing all ten answers!

Don't underestimate the power of this quiz. It will bring great truth to the surface in your life. It is such a powerful exercise, in fact, that a second copy of the quiz is in the addendum, for you to use at a later time.

Top 10 Ways
to Love Myself Perfectly
Self-quiz

If I were loving myself perfectly, I would:

1. _____

2. _____

3. _____

4. _____

5. _____

6. _____

7. _____

8. _____

9. _____

10. _____

***What you have listed above is
the love you deserve***
—
from yourself

What happened when I took the quiz myself?

When I answered the *Top 10 Ways to Love Myself Perfectly* quiz myself, I was rather surprised at what came out. Here were some of my answers:

If I were loving myself perfectly, I would:

♦ Feel no fear or doubt about income flow as I changed occupations to writer and speaker.

♦ Give myself generous time to write this book even though there were thousands of other demands on my time.

♦ Affirm to myself that the message in this book was from divine Love, not from me personally.

♦ Affirm to myself that this book would speak to the hearts of humanity with great comfort and liberation.

♦ Boldly implement my heart-directed lifepath without doubt or guilt.

I was shocked that there were so many ways that I *wasn't* loving myself perfectly. I became instantly aware of how much fear, doubt, and guilt still existed in my private consciousness as I thought about my life and how tentative I was in putting my passion – writing this book – in first place in my life.

The result of taking my own quiz was dramatic and propelled me into high gear. I decided once and for all to leave fear and guilt in the dust and move forward openly and joyously with my passion –

writing this book to you. With Shannon's encouraging support, I gave this book first place in my life and began to boldly walk my treasured lifepath.

The next day I invited 25 people to be on a review team for the book. Even though this book was only half written, I decided to surround myself with a team that would honor and support me – and light a fire under me! I knew this would be a potent way of loving myself – and loving this book. By committing myself to 25 people that I highly respected, I knew I would be forced to complete the book rapidly. I also knew I would be openly exposing what I had written to a test audience and, for better or worse, that would get this book completed at the highest level of clarity.

Within two months, to my great surprise, I finished the second half of this book. You are now holding the result of my loving myself enough to take my own medicine and love myself perfectly.

Imagine the impact on the world and our lovelives if every person reading this book took a bold stand for loving themselves.

Loving yourself
is a
bold affirmation
of the value
of your
life

The value
of identifying
the top 10 ways
to love yourself perfectly

Envision how you would feel if you *were* loving yourself perfectly? You would feel:

♦ Joyous.

♦ Liberated.

♦ Satisfied.

♦ Self-empowered.

♦ Ready to expand and grow and give.

♦ Ready to unleash the vastness of your potential.

♦ Ready to give and receive love at a much higher level.

Think of the benefits this would bring to your love-mate. Not only would your love-mate feel your self-empowered, self-loving energy, but you would be encouraging your love-mate to complete the same *Top 10 Ways to Love Myself Perfectly* quiz and join in the liberation!

Not
loving yourself
creates disaster in your love-life

We must face the truth:

♦ If you are depressed, sullen, morose, frustrated, angry, or withdrawn, you will bring misery to yourself and your love-mate.

♦ If you are allowing yourself to be abused by a love-mate by accepting ridicule, put-downs, name-calling, blaming, condemnation, manipulation, or unkindness, then love will be sucked out of your environment.

♦ If you are living in false hope that your love-mate will soon begin loving you with the love you deserve – even though it has been days, weeks, months, years, or never, you are depriving *yourself* of love.

We all know this, but we easily overlook and accept these conditions. We need to step decisively outside these unacceptable limitations to the love we deserve.

Of course we feel enormous compassion for those suffering from the inability or unwillingness to heal their anger, depression, or unkindness, but we must draw a line that preserves our own dignity.

Loving yourself
calls for
self-honoring
that does not
enable or tolerate abuse

This is a lot easier to say than to do. We may wonder how a good friend, relative, or parent, could possibly allow herself/himself to remain trapped in love-misery – unless we have experienced this ourselves and felt the quiet terror of daring to even think of taking steps towards freedom.

Society has gradually come to regard physical abuse of a love-mate as inexcusable, but far too many love-mates are still faced with emotional or verbal abuse every day of their love-lives. This demeaning environment is *not* love and we must stop accepting or enabling this treatment.

Even though a difficult relationship may seem insurmountable, we must see that it is not a *condition.* It can exist only so long as we tolerate it in consciousness.

> ### The secret
> ### of escaping from love-misery
> ### is to recognize
> ### that the solution
> ### is always
> ### within
> ### you

Let us learn how to love ourselves perfectly so we can enjoy the love we deserve.

Here are some ways:

Rethink your list
of the top 10 ways
to love yourself perfectly

Go to some private spot that feels like a sanctuary and allow yourself, in utter stillness, to *feel* the idea of loving yourself perfectly.

Then rethink and refine your answers to the *Top 10 Ways to Love Myself Perfectly* quiz.

Ask yourself:

> **What are the
> highest possible ways
> I can
> love myself
> right now?**

Many of us live so far below this level of loving ourselves that we do not even *think* down this beautiful road. We are so accustomed to accepting less. We stay locked into habits of thought.

But these habits can be changed!

Those of you reading this book who are living in the midst of love-abuse or love-misery will be tempted to exclude yourself from the possibility of loving yourself. I know. I have been in that spot.

Yet loving yourself is the way out of misery – even misery that seems beyond our control.

> **Loving yourself
> is the path
> to
> freedom**

Quietly take time to envision what you have written.

Let yourself feel and appreciate what you have identified.

Congratulate yourself for coming this far. Writing out your list is an empowering step towards the love you deserve.

Affirm

that you deserve

to love yourself perfectly

Right now, as I write this chapter to you, I am sitting in my car – alone in a quiet corner of a park full of tall trees and disappearing trails. It is sprinkling ever so lightly. I came here to be in touch with loving myself – and loving you – while I wrote this chapter. My computer is on my lap and I am quietly listening to Love for guidance.

Let me share some affirmations, as they come to me. As you read them, think of them as affirmations about *you*:

> *"I know that loving myself acknow-ledges my oneness – my being at one with divine Love. I am Love's creation and Love's expression.*
>
> *I know that loving myself is a bold affirmation and expression of Love itself and empowers not only me, but also my love-mate – because what blesses one blesses everyone.*
>
> *I know that all mankind deserves to see itself as united in Love – loved and loving. I am envisioning all mankind in this perfect unity with Love and cherishing this as mankind's right!"*

Post
your top 10 list

Post your top 10 list where you will see it all the time. Think of this list as:

- Your *most important* assignment in life.
- A Love-given opportunity.
- What you can do today to live at your highest level of identity.
- The greatest gift you can give yourself.

Don't let your list slide into oblivion. Let that list jump out at you from your mirror, brief case, computer, purse, wallet, or car and say:

"Hey, it's time to love myself with the love I deserve – and here's how!"

If your goals seem too big to implement, put one small section into action – right now!

**Transformation
begins with a
single
step**

Notice how many items on your list do not depend on anyone but *you*!

**No one can
stop you
from loving yourself
–
except you!**

Spend

one day

loving yourself perfectly

Suppose you were shopping for clothes with a friend who was a great judge of how to make you look great, and she said,

"Here, try this on. You'd look fantastic in this."

Even if you couldn't *imagine* such a new look, you might try it on just to see.

Or suppose a respected friend suggested a new line of work for you based on your talents and qualities. You might feel resistance to such a new idea and it might seem overwhelming to think down a whole new lifepath.

Yet during our lifetimes, we all change our physical looks – and occupations. And, often, when we take that first new step, it seems like a gigantic adjustment.

Look back on how you looked ten years ago, or what you did as an occupation.

Have you changed?

Amazing!

So... can you spare *one* day to practice loving yourself perfectly?

In whatever way you have been living – whether hating yourself, stuck in a difficult love relationship, wallowing in self-doubt, or wondering if you'll ever be truly loved – let that all go for 24 hours:

- Get that *Top 10 Ways to Love Myself Perfectly* list out and start living it.

- Let yourself *experience* loving yourself perfectly for one day. (If you insist, you can always return to old habits of guilt, doubt, or fear tomorrow.)

Wouldn't you encourage your son, daughter, best friend, or love-mate to take this step?

Let yourself
live
in the embrace
of Love
right now!

Share your list
with your love-mate

Sharing your list with your love-mate:

♦ Shows your love-mate your commitment to loving yourself.

♦ Makes your answers more real – even to yourself.

♦ Affirms to *you* that your answers are important.

♦ Creates more intimacy with your love-mate, allowing you to connect at the core of your being.

♦ Enables your love-mate to know what is in your consciousness, and how to support you more effectively.

If you are in a difficult relationship with a love-mate, it may not be easy or possible to share your list. So be it!

Don't let that stop you from practicing your list and loving yourself forward. Recognize what a great step you have already taken. The fact that you have taken the time to identify how to love yourself perfectly will raise you to a new level in your love relationship because you will have far more clarity about what you deserve.

The real issue is not whether your love relationship will improve or dissolve. The larger issue is that you will be more united to divine Love and therefore closer to what Love has in store for you – and that's the love you deserve!

***Loving yourself
unites you with Love***

Align
yourself with Love

Loving yourself in all the ways discussed in this chapter brings you closer to the heart of perfect love – aligns you to Love:

♦ You feel freer to express your honest feelings and desires.

♦ You connect with greater intimacy with your love-mate because you are no longer hiding your true self.

♦ You find *yourself* being more loving and more loveable.

♦ You experience communication, inter-actions, and love-making with your love-mate at a spiritual level of unity.

♦ You feel united with Love and experience the joy of living out from the love you deserve.

Aligning yourself
with Love
connects you to the heart
of
the love you deserve

Chapter 11

Loving out
from spirituality

Millennium consciousness is bursting forth from the heart of spirituality.

Spirituality is our awareness of a Higher Power – a sense of being at one with this Power, whatever we name it – God, Creator, Infinite One, Light, Spirit, Truth, Principle, Mind, Soul, Life, or divine Love.

Spirituality is the understanding that this Higher Power has created us and expresses us.

Spirituality is the consciousness that God *is* Love and that we are the expression of this infinite Love.

This is the great truth that illumines why perfect love is possible:

Perfect love is possible
because divine Love
is the source
of the love
we express and experience

We do not create love. Love creates and expresses us.

We are not acquiring love. We are discovering Love.

We are not climbing *towards* love. We are living *out from* Love.

We are not becoming spiritual

We are spiritual

Once we enter this consciousness of spiritual Love, our love lives totally refocus:

♦ We redefine *ourselves* as purely spiritual, hence purely loving.

♦ We see our love-mates as spiritual and the expression of spiritual Love.

♦ We see our love-relationship as a spiritual event and union.

♦ We see that no one can possibly be excluded from infinite, universal Love.

♦ We open our hearts and minds to the embrace of infinite Love.

We all feel the energy of this spiritual awakening. Some may no longer turn to churches, institutions, social groups, or even family members for spiritual answers, but we are looking within. We are buying books on spirituality, meditating privately, and discovering our spirituality in our own way.

And we are all arriving at the same point in consciousness:

Spirituality
is our essence

–

our core substance

Spirituality is no longer an important *portion* of our identity. We are learning that spirituality *is* our *complete* identity.

This revelation is as paradigm-shattering as Einstein's consciousness which changed the way we perceived our universe. The universe did not change with Einstein. Our *consciousness* changed and that changed our world. Today, another revolution is taking place in thought:

Spirituality
is the
paradigm-shattering revolution
taking place today
in
consciousness

It may seem that some of us have spirituality in our love lives and some of us do not, but this is a mistaken view.

Spirituality
is the central principle
of our love lives
whether we see it or not

All the love you have ever known, or ever will know, is already within you. You already include this love.

***Spirituality
is the core
of all the love
we will ever experience
– forever –
with anyone***

If we are ignorant of spirituality, this does not make the spiritual nature of our being less true. Ignorance only hides spirituality from our view and experience. We are all living at different stages of *discovering* spiritual love as our inherent identity.

***Awareness
of our spirituality
enables us
to experience
the infinite nature
of all-empowering Love***

Let us become aware of spirituality as the force of Love guiding our love-lives.

Here are some ways that will enable you to see your love-life in its spiritual light:

Recognize
the 10 keys to perfect love
as ways of expressing
spiritual Love

With the higher view of spirituality *as* Love, think again of what you have read so far in this book.

Each of the 10 keys to perfect love shows a tangible way of expressing the nature and power of spiritual Love.

- ◆ A **bond of unity** is the natural, inevitable outcome of spirituality and Love.

- ◆ **Kindness + honesty** express the essence of Love and spirituality in action.

- ◆ **Cherishing each other's dreams** demonstrates the infinite, honoring nature of Love.

- ◆ Could spirituality or Love allow anything less than **genuine equality** for both love-mates?

- ◆ As we **listen to each other's hearts**, we are listening *as* Love.

- ◆ **Perpetual intimacy** is the 'joyous, natural, effortless result of spiritual union.

- ◆ **Manhood** which **empowers others** is synonymous with all-empowering Love.

- ◆ **Self-empowered womanhood** acknowledges the completeness and authority of divine Love.

- ♦ **Loving yourself perfectly** esteems your true identity as the idea of Love.
- ♦ **Loving out from spirituality** unites us with our true identity as the nature and expression of infinite Love.

Doesn't this spiritual vision of the love you deserve take you to glorious, empowering heights!

> *Rather than*
> *searching for love*
> *in thousands of places and moments,*
> *look out from Love*
> *and know that you are already there*

As the poet Rumi so eloquently told us many centuries ago:

> *The minute I heard my first love story*
> *I started looking for you, not knowing*
> *how blind that was.*
>
> *Lovers don't finally meet somewhere.*
> *They're in each other all along.*

With our growing spiritual awareness today, we can all know:

> *The love I deserve*
> *is within me*
> *because I*
> *express & experience*
> *Love's*
> *completeness*

See

identity

as spiritual, not physical

***By seeing
real identity
as spiritual, not physical,
we see
with the eyes of Love***

Think of all the love relationships you have observed in your life.

Which is the best relationship you have ever witnessed? Describe this relationship in five separate words or phrases:

1. _____
2. _____
3. _____
4. _____
5. _____

Here is my answer. The best relationship I have ever witnessed was between my mother and father. The way I would describe their relationship to you in five words or phrases is:

1. Consistently kind.
2. Unconditionally loving.
3. Radically spiritual.
4. Joyous and happy.
5. Embracing others with open love.

Do you know how tall my mother was? How much my father weighed? What color eyes they had? No!

Suppose I had described my Mom and Dad's relationship to you this way:

1. 5' 9" in love with 5"2."
2. 170 pounds mated with 120 pounds.
3. Size 9 feet dancing with size 6 feet.
4. Blue eyes looking at hazel eyes.
5. Grey hair in love with brown hair.

Which description of my Mom and Dad lets you meet them most accurately?

Real identity cannot be described physically

—

real identity is spiritual

How about your description? Did you describe spiritual qualities or physical appearance?

Now, take this exercise yet another step and uncover *your* true identity. Describe your spiritual identity in five words or phrases.

1. _____
2. _____
3. _____
4. _____
5. _____

Your spiritual identity is what makes you irresistibly attractive & loveable

Love out
from spirituality

The summit of spiritual consciousness is to recognize that you are not *searching for love*, but already *loving out from Love*.

It does not matter whether you are single, struggling in love, or happy in love. What matters is that you think, live, and love out from the summit of spiritual consciousness.

*When you
see yourself
as purely spiritual
and act out from Love,
perfect love
will flow into your life*

Loving out from Love is radically empowering – to you and your love-mate.

To love *out from* Love, rather than struggling *up to* Love, forces you to drop guilt, fear, doubt, and low self-worth and adopt a consciousness that knows that Love and you are one. Envision yourself loving out from Love and thinking:

*"Love
is expressing itself to the world
as me*

—

*I feel Love's
presence and power
as
my nature and expression"*

Here is the spiritual truth about you:

♦ You are Love's nature – incapable of expressing anything less than perfect Love.

♦ You are Love's ambassador – assigned to represent Love accurately.

♦ You are Love's idea – sent to show your love-mate, and all others in your life, by your actions, what Love feels like.

If you catch yourself saying, *"I don't think I can do that,"* you are correct because "you" are not the one doing the loving.

Love is doing the loving!

You are the expression, not the creator. Open yourself to your unity with Love and let Love express itself perfectly *as* you.

Act with the gentleness and patience of Love.

Act with the authority of Love.

Act **as** Love.

Divine Love
is
expressing, defining,
cherishing, enabling, and leading
you
to
the love you deserve

Moving

towards

perfect love

Chapter 12

Single and without a love-mate

If you are single, separated, or divorced and without a love-mate, consider yourself *blessed and fortunate* rather than forsaken.

> ***You have an***
> ***advanced opportunity***
> ***right now***
> ***to get love***
> ***right!***

As some of you may know from experience, getting out of an unhappy relationship, or marriage, is a whole lot harder and more painful than getting into the relationship. Even when we do exit a bad relationship, many of us promptly leap yet again into another unfulfilling relationship.

What does it take to learn?

Here are some clear steps that will move you towards the love you deserve:

Seize
the opportunity
to establish your own
love-standard

"I had almost given up hope that the love described in this book was possible. The 10 keys so beautifully articulated are my new measuring stick for all future love-mates. I'm no longer willing to compromise."

That's what one young woman decided after reading this book.

Even if you have no lover in sight, recognize this fulfilling truth:

Your consciousness
establishes
the quality of love
you
experience

Use this book to set and establish your own love-standards.

Don't
compromise
the love you deserve!

Discuss
this book
with potential love-mates

You will be amazed at how quickly you get to know a friend or potential love-mate through discussing this book.

For example, suppose your potential love-mate responds to this idea with one of the following statements:

♦ *"I'm not interested in books on love."*

♦ *"These books are all the same. They are only trying to force me to change from who I am."*

♦ *"I'd love to discuss this book together. I want to love you well and I want to be well-loved."*

Which of these love-prospects is still in your life?

If you can't discuss a book on perfect love with a potential love-mate, how likely are you to experience perfect love with that person?

Practice loving
perfectly

If you were an astronaut, you would practice and practice and practice before you were sent into space.

Would you fly in a plane with a pilot that was not trained, or use a lawyer that had not studied law?

Yet how many of us have taken a single course – in our entire lives – on how to succeed in love!

***Envision this book as
an advanced training program
designed to make you an
expert in loving***

Your practice will do even more than make you a great love-mate. Your consciousness will be so transformed by your advanced training and practice, that potential love-mates who are seeking the same quality of love will be attracted to you.

They will recognize you.

And – just as importantly – *you* will recognize them.

One woman, after reading this book, recognized that one of her best friends fit her new sense of love-mate far more closely than those she was dating. Her expanding consciousness of perfect love is changing her experience.

Think of yourself
as right now
loving
your future love-mate

Somewhere, right now, your future love-mate is being prepared for you.

You, too, are being prepared.

Ask yourself:

♦ How well am I loving?

♦ How conscious am I of the ten keys to perfect love?

♦ Am I practicing the ten keys with my friends and dates?

♦ Am I an expert at loving perfectly?

Challenge yourself to become an expert at loving your future love-mate *right now*:

♦ Realize that perfect love is *within you*.

♦ Affirm that perfect love is your *right*.

♦ Practice loving your future love-mate.

♦ Experience being at one with Love.

♦ Live this book.

♦ Love *out from*, not up to Love.

♦ Express yourself *as* Love.

***Learning
to love perfectly
is the most advanced opportunity
you have
right now
to move towards
the love you deserve***

Feel yourself experiencing perfect love before it occurs

♦ *Admit* the possibility of experiencing perfect love.

♦ *Cherish* perfect love as your inherent *right*.

♦ *Envision* yourself as *already* in the embrace of perfect love.

This consciousness is not wishful or positive thinking. This consciousness is the inevitable awakening to your spiritual *right* to experience perfect love.

You *already* have this right.

As you open yourself to this right, you will find yourself experiencing and enjoying the consciousness of perfect love.

*The
spiritual consciousness
of
perfect love
knows
that Love includes
its own
fulfillment*

Chapter 13

Happy with a love-mate
but
open to more

The key here is "open to more."

If you and your love-mate are *eager* to expand your love – or simply *willing* to expand your love – that says a lot of good about the quality of your love.

> ***To be open***
> ***to more love***
> ***shows an understanding***
> ***that Love***
> ***is***
> ***infinite***

Here are some ways that will open you to the infinite possibilities of Love:

Read

the previous chapter

Single and without a love-mate

Even though you already have a love-mate, review the chapter, *Single and without a love-mate,* to establish a new base of consciousness from which to grow:

♦   Did you miss any of the recommended steps?

♦   Did you bring perfect love to your relationship?

♦   Are you expressing perfect love today?

***Perfect love
is like a river***

—

***never static
always flowing and carving
out new life***

Read this book
together
and share your feelings

Sharing feelings is easier for women.

Several of the men on my review team privately acknowledged how difficult it is for them to share their feelings. It was not that they are unreceptive to sharing. They are simply inexperienced in sharing.

Yet these men not only read this book, but shared the experience with their love-mates.

This is all the opening that perfect love needs.

Perfect love
is like brilliant light
that sneaks through the cracks
in our consciousness
when we open ourselves to growth

—

we can never return
to darkness

Set

new standards

for your relationship

As you share your feelings with each other, use this book to set new standards for your relationship:

- ♦ Share your answers together *on The Love You Deserve* quiz.
- ♦ Go through each of *the 10 Keys to Perfect Love* and openly identify and discuss your feelings, needs, and desires.
- ♦ Identify what would move your love relationship to a 10 in each key.
- ♦ Identify how you can help each other grow.

Give

gratitude

Gratitude makes the heart sing.

You cannot overdo gratitude.

Make a list right now of the 10 ways that you most value your love-mate:

1. _____

2. _____

3. _____

4. _____

5. _____

6. _____

7. _____

8. _____

9. _____

10. _____

Does your love-mate know about this list? It shouldn't be a secret.

On one of our anniversaries (we count them by months) I gave my wife a binder titled "48 reasons I love Shannon." Some were small. Some were large. Here are some of them:

Some of the reasons
I love Shannon

- ♥ She is my best, most wonderful friend.
- ♥ Her support is stronger than all the Sumo wrestlers in the world.
- ♥ She dances with delight and freedom.
- ♥ She speaks with wonderful, nurturing, healing love to the whole world.
- ♥ She calls me "Sweetie." I try to ignore this, of course, because she calls about 22,345 other people "Sweetie" too.
- ♥ Her prayers lift me to heights of glorious awareness never before imagined.
- ♥ She imitates opera singers with outlandish taste, vigor, noise, and hilarity. "ALFREDO. I LOVE YOU!"
- ♥ She puts her arm over my neck when we walk.
- ♥ She expresses the joy and freedom of Soul.
- ♥ She is a full-time, happy, powerful Christian Science practitioner with 17 years of healings that are supporting the universe.
- ♥ Her eyes sparkle with love and delight.
- ♥ She is totally spontaneous.
- ♥ She teases me mercilessly.
- ♥ She has the full complement of tennis equipment – large storage bag, mini-storage bag, balls, racket, cute, color-coordinated outfits – and, occasionally, we even play tennis.
- ♥ She understands equality, believes in it, and seeks to live it.
- ♥ She has the courage to be completely honest with me. What a joy!

- ♥ She empowers me. She liberates me. I find my real, desired self in her presence.
- ♥ She paints impressionistically. I love her works.
- ♥ She thinks from the mountain-top of divine Mind and lives from the mountain-top of divine Love.
- ♥ She laughs and laughs and laughs. Pure joy!
- ♥ She loves to collide hugging me.
- ♥ She hasn't tickled my feet for several months.
- ♥ She gently moves back and forth from problems to solutions, lifting thought higher while simultaneously laughing, knowing, and acknowledging felt needs.
- ♥ She loves me with passion and creativity.
- ♥ She is joyously playful and laughs at herself.
- ♥ She is wonderfully profuse in her expression of ideas. Ideas gush from her consciousness. She exudes. Her creativity is endless. She is the constant release of abundance. Her expression overflows. She rushes, surges, swells, flows, streams, spills, spews, and spurts with fascinating, novel, unusual, creative ideas. Well, you get the idea.
- ♥ She leaves kind, intelligent, up-to-the-minute messages on her voice mail.
- ♥ She writes with vigor, clarity, and intelligence.
- ♥ She is a waterfall of creativity and originality.
- ♥ She is real.
- ♥ She thinks without limitations.
- ♥ She sparkles.
- ♥ She refuses to accept less than God's answer on any issue.
- ♥ She loves me!

Identify

more ways of being intimate

Intimacy brings us to the heart of perfect love.

What are 10 ways that you – *acting on your own* – can bring more intimacy to your relationship?

1. _____
2. _____
3. _____
4. _____
5. _____
6. _____
7. _____
8. _____
9. _____
10. _____

What are 10 ways that – *together with your love-mate* – you can bring more intimacy to your relationship?

1. _____
2. _____
3. _____
4. _____
5. _____
6. _____
7. _____
8. _____
9. _____
10. _____

Practice

perfect love

Give yourself the advanced assignment of practicing the love described in this book.

Take this book to heart and start living the 10 keys to perfect love.

These keys are not abstract or theoretical. They are practical, straight-forward, and easy to understand.

- ◆ Don't let pride, frustration, lack of patience, or "You go first" stop you from being a perfect lover.
- ◆ Rate yourself on your expertise with each of the 10 keys.
- ◆ Practice on your weak areas with the commitment to becoming an expert.
- ◆ Love yourself as you grow.

***Only
the practice of
loving
makes us
expert lovers***

Chapter 14

Struggling for happiness with a love-mate

If I had read this book during either of my previous marriages, I would have been silently mourning, thinking to myself:

> *"I'll never experience such love. I'm immersed in a relationship with little hope of fulfillment, not to mention perfect love."*

Yet today, I am writing to you from the heart of the experience of perfect love.

Was I a failure?

No!

I was simply not awake to perfect love. I did not have the consciousness, commitment, conviction, and authority to act out from perfect love – and to accept nothing less.

Were either of my ex-wives failures?

No!

None of us were awake to perfect love.

There were loving moments, but the idea of our *right* to perfect love, grounded in spirituality, was not established.

Yet all that time I was being prepared and loved by Love:

- This book could not have come forth without the experience of *failed* love.
- This book could not have come forth without the experience of *perfect* love.
- I give gratitude today for these experiences in love.
- I feel great compassion for those currently struggling for happiness with a love-mate.
- I now understand, with the spiritual authority that comes from being at one with Love, that perfect love belongs to *each* of us.

Here are some ways to move to higher ground in your love-life:

Decide

right now

that there *is* a solution

Solutions come to us in unexpected ways.

Do you know the story of the man whose house was flooding? A neighbor in a boat came to rescue him, but he declined the help, saying:

"God will save me!"

The flood waters rose and soon the man had to climb to his second floor to stay above the water line. Another rescue boat arrived. He shouted:

"No thanks. God will save me!"

But the waters kept rising. Standing on his roof with flood waters almost washing his house away, a helicopter let down its rescue ladder. But the man wouldn't take it.

He soon drowned in the waters.

Arriving in heaven, he asked:

"Why would God not save me?"

And God replied:

"Well, I sent two boats and a helicopter!"

We need to be alert to solutions. If we don't expect one, or if we have pre-determined what the solution must be, we are unlikely to see it when it arrives.

Perhaps this book is part of your spiritual solution.

Unlike the man in the flood who had little understanding of God, you can look out from a mental position that acknowledges God as infinite Love.

With this spiritual awareness, you feel the embrace of Love:

- ♦   You are not trapped.
- ♦   This is your opportunity to grow.
- ♦   Expect to be loved.
- ♦   Don't refuse Love's embrace.
- ♦   Let Love open the way for you.
- ♦   Be alert to *Love's* solution!

***When
we
acknowledge
the power of Love
we open ourselves to
Love's
presence***

See
yourself
as worthy of perfect love

It is often difficult to see yourself as lovely and loveable when you are struggling with an intimate relationship.

It is even harder if your love-mate is not being kind to you, or not valuing you.

***Never think
that you are unworthy
simply because you are being
treated as unworthy
by a love-mate***

♦ Affirm your right to perfect love.

♦ Reread the chapter on *Loving yourself perfectly*.

♦ Implement your *Top 10 Ways to Love Myself Perfectly* list.

♦ Surround yourself with people who cherish your worth.

♦ Start loving yourself!

***Stay awake
to your
loveliness!***

Affirm perfect love

for

everyone

As you start loving yourself more perfectly, include everyone you know in your meditations, prayers, or thoughts.

Affirm that everything written in this book belongs not just to you, but to every single one of your friends, family members, and loved ones.

When you have finished embracing every friend, family member, and loved one in the consciousness of Love, affirm Love's presence for everyone you *don't know* in the world.

This consciousness breaks us free of the tight, mental confines of our own love relationship.

By embracing
all
mankind
in our affirmations of Love,
we see
into our own love-lives
with
greater clarity

Reach out
to your love-mate
with perfect love

Growth is often invisible and easy to overlook.

Just think how much struggle and growth is taking place within your private consciousness right now – that only you know about. Much of what is stirring within you may seem hard, even impossible, to talk about with others or your love-mate.

This same growth is taking place within *all* of us – even within your love-mate.

Don't be fooled
into thinking
that someone is not growing
because you cannot
see it

Growth first takes place in consciousness, and then in action. With this awareness, reach out to your love-mate with all the skills you have learned in this book.

- ♦ Tell your love-mate that you want to grow together positively, not negatively.
- ♦ Ask your love-mate to read and discuss this book with you. Ask with kindness + honesty. Do it *as* Love, not as a threat.
- ♦ Work to create an environment of kindness + honesty.

♦ Love your love-mate the way you would like to be loved in the same situation.

♦ Be open in discussing your needs and desires with your love-mate. Don't be afraid. Love is expressing you. Ask for your love-mate's support.

♦ Ask your love-mate what he or she would most like from you to improve the relationship.

♦ Demonstrate listening, cherishing, and honoring of your love-mate.

♦ See your love-mate as spiritual. You may have entirely different views, but affirming that your love-mate is spiritual will enable you to speak to the highest good within your love-mate.

Speak to the King or Queen
within your love-mate
and the
King or Queen
will
come forth

Set

a standard

for the love you deserve

Whether your love-mate is responsive or not, set a standard for the love *you* deserve.

If your love-mate does not care about your love needs, the real issue is not your love-mate's attitude, but whether *you* are willing to accept a lower standard of love than you deserve.

With all that you have invested in your love relationship, it is natural to try to raise your relationship to your new awareness of perfect love, rather than to simply walk away.

This is an opportunity not to condemn your love-mate, but to lovingly explain a higher standard of love that can reward each of you.

But it is also an opportunity to love yourself enough to be honest with your love-mate about your needs and desires.

If, after you have won a gold medal for your skills of communicating to your love-mate with honesty + kindness, your partner still expresses no interest in growing, you have to ask the tough questions:

- ♦ Is this really love?
- ♦ Am I willing to accept this lower standard of "love" for the rest of my life?
- ♦ Am I staying in the relationship because I feel pity for my love-mate? Or fear of what might happen?
- ♦ Do I love myself enough to take a stand for perfect love?

"But I'll be all alone if I leave," you may fear.

The truth is that if you stay in such a relationship, you will be alone – very alone. The long-term pain of staying in the relationship may be worse that the pain of separation.

Before you contemplate this stand, surround yourself with friends that love you, keep practicing your perfect love skills with your love-mate, and listen keenly to your intuition.

Build

a support team

We need friends around us who honor us, see us as loveable, and help awaken us to our inner worth.

I failed to do this during my previous marriages – perhaps because I am a man. Although I now recognize how obvious my struggle was to others, it was difficult for me to confide in anyone. I thought of this as not being loyal to my wife.

I now realize how self-destructive this was. My failure to surround myself with friends who could love me and encourage me to be open, kept me imprisoned in my own private struggle.

My self-isolation also kept me from hearing good things about myself and I began to seriously doubt my worth.

Love yourself
enough
to surround yourself
with friends
who will
listen, cherish, honor, esteem, and
support your worth

Don't
have an affair

It is only natural that during a struggle for happiness with a love-mate, you might be tempted to seek love with another who seems more loving, but having an affair while you are married:

♦ Does not solve your love problems. It worsens them. It prevents you from moving forward effectively with either relationship.

♦ Avoids the real issue of facing up to your love-mate and taking steps towards healing – whether that means working to improve your relationship, or separating.

♦ Violates your right to perfect love because you will be forced to act without kindness + honesty to your partner – and will not be loving out from spirituality.

Love yourself enough
to bring
your present relationship
to resolution
or
closure

Trust
your intuition

A spiritual mentor, an expert on healing, once told me a valuable truth:

"Never give advice."

As much as we may think we know what is right for another person, it is not our place in the universe to tell another person what decision to make.

Although this book is loaded with ideas, it is your decision to accept or reject them.

Our highest position of loving another person is to affirm that divine Love is upholding and leading that person – and to provide all the listening, cherishing, and honoring we know how to give.

And, even more importantly:

> ***The highest position
> we can take
> in loving ourselves
> is to trust
> our
> own intuition***

Intuition is prayer.

As we listen quietly and unreservedly to Love, we will hear Love's truth speaking directly to our consciousness.

Be the one
to execute the vision

All of us have personal insights on the best way to accomplish a goal or dream that is important to us. Yet we often seek the approval of others before we act. I have spent many frustrating moments trying to convince others of my deeply felt ideas.

My insightful wife Shannon, however, has taught me a great truth about vision. One day, she simply said:

> *The person
> with the vision
> has to execute
> the vision*

This truth has forever changed me. I now realize the power of executing my own vision and letting others either adopt it or not.

As I reach the end of this book in the privacy of writing out my vision of perfect love, I have already achieved my goal. I have openly stated my vision, and I have done so without asking if others approve. I have shared the song of my heart – as a gift to you.

You, too, must sing your song!

Your love-mate does not control your song. When struggling for happiness in a relationship, we may be tempted to want our love-mate to be the one to change, but the higher, more powerful approach is to dig into our own intuition for our vision of what we want and need – and then execute this vision ourselves.

For example, after six years in a previous marriage that had good moments, but was unhappy for both of us, I wrestled my way towards a clear vision. After years of hoping that the love I thought I was expressing would result in a transformed marriage, I realized my mistake. I was waiting for my wife to change rather than taking a stand for what I knew in my intuition was right for me.

I remember walking down the hall in our home and saying to my wife:

> *"We need to commit to improving our*
> *marriage, or else end our marriage.*
> *Do you want to work on it?"*

To my surprise, she said *"No."* But the honesty of this moment and my willingness to execute the vision I knew was right, led to an amicable divorce. I had taken a step towards the love I deserved. And so had she.

> ***Know***
> ***that during every moment***
> ***you struggle for happiness***
> ***in a relationship,***
> ***you are not***
> ***alone***

Your friends are with you. I am with you. Thousands of people are supporting you with love that you cannot see. Most importantly:

> ***Love itself***
> ***is cherishing you***
> ***and***
> ***leading you***
> ***to***
> ***the love you deserve***

You have now entered the embrace of perfect love

You have come to the last page of this book.

More importantly, however, you have now entered the embrace of perfect love.

Nothing
can stop or prevent
the spiritual illumination
and steady unfolding
of
perfect love in your life
– for eternity –
because you are
divine Love's expression
and now
you know it!

As the empowering spiritual healer, Mary Baker Eddy, said so concisely:

"No power can withstand divine Love."

We can
never retreat
from a consciousness
that has
seen the light

Final self-quiz
Your ideal love-mate

Directions: Now that you have completed *The Love You Deserve: 10 Keys to Perfect Love,* write your answers again to the question below. Don't look back at your answers at the beginning of the book until you have finished.

The top 10 things I want in a love-mate:

1. _____

2. _____

3. _____

4. _____

5. _____

6. _____

7. _____

8. _____

9. _____

10. _____

Has your love consciousness changed as a result of reading this book?

Addendum

The Love You Deserve
Self-quiz

Directions: If you currently have a love-mate, circle the number that best describes your relationship. If you don't have a love-mate at this time, circle the lowest rating you are willing to accept with any love-mate-to-be.

1.   I feel a bond of unity with my love-mate:

  1   2   3   4   5   6   7   8   9   10

Not at all   To some degree   Completely

2.   I am treated with consistent kindness and honesty by my love-mate:

  1   2   3   4   5   6   7   8   9   10

Not at all   To some degree   Completely

3.   My love-mate cherishes my dreams:

  1   2   3   4   5   6   7   8   9   10

Not at all   To some degree   Completely

4.   I experience genuine equality with my love-mate in all aspects of our relationship:

  1   2   3   4   5   6   7   8   9   10

Not at all   To some degree   Completely

5.   My love-mate listens to my heart:

  1   2   3   4   5   6   7   8   9   10

Not at all   To some degree   Completely

6.   I experience perpetual intimacy with my love-mate:

  1   2   3   4   5   6   7   8   9   10

Not at all   To some degree   Completely

7. My love-mate honors and supports empowering manhood:

    1   2   3   4   5   6   7   8   9   10

Not at all   To some degree   Completely

8. My love-mate honors and supports empowered womanhood:

    1   2   3   4   5   6   7   8   9   10

Not at all   To some degree   Completely

9. I love myself perfectly:

    1   2   3   4   5   6   7   8   9   10

Not at all   To some degree   Completely

10. I am loving out from spirituality:

    1   2   3   4   5   6   7   8   9   10

Not at all   To some degree   Completely

Self-Rating

Total Score: _____ divided by 10 = _____

1-2 Love vacuum. Time for radical revision or new possibilities.

3-4 Minimal love. Time to set higher standards.

5-6 Survivable love. Is this acceptable to you for the rest of your life?

7-8 Decent love. Why not go for the gold? What would move you to a 10?

9-10 Perfect love. Rejoice!

Top 10 Ways
to Love Myself Perfectly
Self-quiz

If I were loving myself perfectly, I would:

1. _____

2. _____

3. _____

4. _____

5. _____

6. _____

7. _____

8. _____

9. _____

10. _____

What you have listed above is
the love you deserve
—
from yourself

S cott Peck conducts workshops and gives talks that empower men and women to experience a higher level of self-worth, spiritual purpose, and love. Peck, who holds a Masters degree in Education, has also served as a reporter for *The Christian Science Monitor*, an advertising manager, management consultant, educator, and real estate broker. He and his wife Shannon live in San Diego, California.

For more information

Responses to this book

Responses to this book are appreciated. If this book has had a significant impact on you or your love life, please write and share your experience.

Audio version

The Love You Deserve is also available on 4 audio cassettes (unabridged) for $29.95 plus tax and handling.

Call toll-free 1-800-266-1525

Credit cards accepted

To contact Scott Peck

To contact Scott Peck to schedule talks or workshops, or to be on the mailing list for future publications, please use one of the following:

Scott Peck
c/o Lifepath Publishing
P. O. Box 830
Solana Beach, CA 92075

1-619-793-8200

E-mail
Scott Peck @AOL.com

Web page
www.ScottPeck.com